GENOCIDE REVEALED

NEW LIGHT ON THE MASSACRE OF SERBS AND JEWS UNDER HUNGARIAN OCCUPATION

GENOCIDE REVEALED

NEW LIGHT ON THE MASSACRE OF SERBS AND JEWS UNDER HUNGARIAN OCCUPATION

BY

ALEKSANDAR VELJIC

Printed in the United States of America
Revised Edition (original edition in 2012 in hardcover format)

Original Serbian works translated and published with permission.

Portions of this book have been published previously in
Miklos Horti-nekaznjeni zlocinac—Copyright 2009 by Aleksandar Veljic, published by Metaphysica, printed in Serbia; and
Istina o Novosadskoj raciji—Copyright 2010 by Aleksandar Veljic, published by Eden, printed in Serbia.

ISBN (hardcover): 978-0-9846938-1-8
ISBN (paperback): 978-1-954102-19-4
ISBN (ebook): 978-1-954102-20-0
Library of Congress Control Number: 2012932843

Edited by Cathy Humble, Caroline C. Minard, Eileen Maddocks, Beth Rule
Cover design by Veronica Coello
Interior design by Amit Dey
Translation from Swedish by Wade Fransson

Published by:
SOMETHING OR OTHER PUBLISHING LLC
Brooklyn, Wisconsin 53521
For general inquiries: Info@SOOPLLC.com
For bulk orders: Orders@SOOPLLC.com

Dedicated to all the victims of genocide

CONTENTS

FOREWORD

Aleksandar Veljic's *Genocide Revealed: New Light on the Massacre of Serbs and Jews under Hungarian Occupation* shines a spotlight on an evil that has hidden in the shadows for eight decades in the ice and snow of Vojvodina. The deliberate mass murder, torture, internment, and deportation of Serbs, Jews, and Roma during World War II by Hungarian Nazi collaborators were carried out with, what the exhaustive work of Veljic has now uncovered, the consent and encouragement of Miklos Horthy, the regent of Hungary, who until this day has never been called before the bar of justice.

In a straightforward manner, Veljic brings to light the diabolical crimes that were part of the Holocaust and reminds us that it was not just the Nazis who committed these horrific acts against humanity, but it was also people from all across Europe, in this case Hungary, who saw others, even their own neighbors, as not like them, and thus not worthy of life, simply because they were different. Veljic's work in uncovering the crimes against humanity that are a part of the Holocaust that took place during World War II must be addressed and not allowed to once again slink into the shadows of darkness. This is a book that everyone should read. Lest we confront our past and learn from it, I fear we are doomed to see it repeated.

—Eric S. Mondschein

PREFACE TO
THE ENGLISH EDITION

For years I have been involved in the research of a little-known genocidal war crime committed in January 1942 in the town where I used to live and its surrounding villages, in what is present-day northern Serbia. What began as a search for information turned into a prolonged investigative process of painstakingly establishing the facts by collecting testimonies and documents.

The more I uncovered about the genocide, called "Razzia" (or *Great Raid*) by the Hungarian occupiers, the more I realized this went far beyond any raid. Labeling atrocities with a lesser name is just one way powerful forces have purposefully and successfully suppressed the truth for eight decades. My own efforts have also been resisted and attempts made to discredit my work. The result is that hundreds of people have become involved in, and have supported, the struggle to publish the book you now hold in your hands.

What makes this work unique? This first-ever English edition compiles published and unpublished Serbian, Jewish, German, Hungarian, and Swedish documentation into a single reference source. It is solidly based on source documents, with attention to names, dates, places, and numbers, and is styled as a historical narrative rather than a stiff presentation of facts and figures.

What makes the Great Raid unique? Whereas the genocide against the European Jews, Slavs, and Roma (once commonly called "Gypsies") was in part so overwhelmingly evil because of the extensive size and scope of the effort—driven by German efficiency, thoroughness, and dispassionate attention to detail—the crimes committed by the Hungarian forces were also atrocious in that gruesome means were used to make the individual suffering more intense, and were implemented by local perpetrators who improvised on the spot in an eagerness to carry out their atrocities. Whereas global attention was brought to bear on the Nazi-led Holocaust in World War II, the Hungarian collaborators who zealously followed their example have managed to hide.

One is continually reminded—despite the phrase *Never Again* which is featured on the gates of Dachau in multiple languages—that unless such crimes are always researched, always called out, always punished, always revealed, they will crop up again and again, wherever hate is allowed to hide in the shadows.

INTRODUCTION

Discussions of fascism usually focus on Mussolini and Hitler, whose national socialism, wars of aggression, devastations, death camps, and genocide are well known. However, a significant personage has eluded collective European consciousness due to the operations of ideological circles that have covered up the consequences of wiping out Serbian, Jewish, Roma, and Slavic peoples.

He is one of the darkest criminals in history, but his crimes remain unknown due to the relatively isolated geography in which they were perpetrated—the Bachka region of northern Serbia.

Uninformed readers and researchers hover stunned over the abyss of the attitudes and atrocities of the agencies—military, gendarmerie, detectives, court martials, office for foreigners, et cetera—generated by this individual.

His followers were heartless. In a series of military actions carried out under his protection, they annihilated those within their grasp who were not of his own cherished ethnicity.

Their arch crime of genocide, named "Razzia" (or *raid, encircling*), was meticulously planned and systematically executed under the direction of this regent in the bitter cold of January 1942.

This work is a depiction of crimes committed by the regent of Hungary, Miklos Horthy, an enemy of humanity who was never brought to justice. The purpose of this book is to bring to light this obscure figure—a murderer whose political career brought great shame upon the Hungarian people as he extinguished thousands of innocent lives.

SECTION I

*The War Crimes of
Miklos Horthy*

RISE TO POWER PRIOR
TO WORLD WAR II

Miklos Horthy (June 18, 1868–February 9, 1957) was the regent of the Kingdom of Hungary from March 1, 1920, to October 15, 1944.

As a young man, Horthy served as a diplomat of the Austro-Hungarian Empire and as a naval aide-de-camp to Emperor Franz Joseph. Later in his career, Horthy became an officer of the Austro-Hungarian navy and served in the Otranto Raid and at the Battle of the Strait of Otranto in 1917. He was Commander in Chief of the Imperial Fleet by the last year of the First World War.

In 1919, Hungarian communists under Béla Kun seized power, proclaiming the Hungarian Soviet Republic and initiating Hungary's Red Terror. In response, a counterrevolutionary government was formed with Horthy in command of its forces.

When the Romanians evacuated Budapest in November 1919, Horthy entered at the head of the National Army. The Hungarian Communist party was banned, and shortly thereafter Horthy was declared Regent and Head of State.

After putting down the Hungarian Soviet Republic, Horthy solidified his power by introducing a bloody terror of torture and murder upon tens of thousands of "laborers, peasants, and Jews."[1] His collaborators appreciated the traits of the up-and-coming regent as expressed in the words of the first Hungarian Prime Minister, Paul Teleky, to a French general: "Horthy is a stout soldier who hates communism infinitely. You can also rely on him for he is going to establish a good order."[2]

The Serbian daily *Politika* reported on September 7, 1919, that Hungary had been conducting a persecution of the Jews under the pretext that they had seduced the working class and wasted the country. The article states: "Certain Hungarian newspapers propagate even a formal extermination of the Jews."[3] Horthy's Hungary was the first European country to call for the annihilation of the Jews, as early as 1919, long predating the Nazis' rise to power.

The terror used by Horthy to establish his regime foreshadowed what was to come—pogroms against those whom he considered undesired elements, who threatened his Nazi-like order.

When Horthy rose to power in 1919, there were 17,132 individuals of Serbian mother tongue in Hungary. By 1930, the Serbian population had dwindled to 7,031 individuals. Only 5,442 Serbs remained in Hungary in 1941.[4]

During the First World War, occupation authorities were set up in the Serbian canton of Zlatibor that extends to the town of Uzhice and its surrounding villages. Locals remembered the evil deeds of the canton occupation commander, Dr. Emerich Nadgy von Shashi. The commander, a future official representative, had sent 976 Uzhice townspeople to the Hungarian camp Nezhider. He conducted particularly intense arrests and deportations of the Serbs to the camp in October 1916. The youngest camp inmates were sixteen years of age; the eldest were sixty. Emerich Nadgy von Shashi sent altogether 271 Zlatibor canton villagers to Nezhider.[5]

In 1932, Gyula Gombosh, the leader of a right-wing party, won elections and became Hungary's prime minister. His political career developed parallel to the rise of German Nazism. The Hungarian public was obsessed with the "Jewish question" as much as with the revision of borders established by the Treaty of Versailles.

Right-wing activists falsely pictured Jews as innately unpatriotic parasites who would undermine national strength and were prone to internationalism (or Bolshevism). Amidst feverish anti-Jewish propaganda, the right-wing parties requested that the Jewish question in Horthy's Hungary be resolved by means of enforcing limitations on the Jewish economic sphere, as well as by "moving Jews out" of the state in an organized fashion.[6]

With Miklos Horthy's blessing, the Hungarian government appointed the Serb-hater Emerich Nadgy von Shashi as justice minister in 1932.[7]

THE FIRST EUROPEAN ANTI-SEMITIC LEADER

Post-Versailles Hungary was obsessed with a couple of national issues: border revision (with aspiration to retrieve territories lost with the disintegration of the Austro-Hungarian Empire), and the Jewish question. In spite of the fact that Hungarian Jewry welcomed assimilation, Jews had never been fully integrated into the Hungarian bourgeoisie class that was oppressive toward Hungarian peasants. Aristocrats used Jews for their political and economic machinations by which they maintained feudal privileges. Impoverished peasantry and industrial workers viewed Jews as an instrument of oppression.[8]

The Hungarian Soviet commune had several prominent Jewish officials led by Béla Kuhn. The main directives of the so-called "Szeged idea" (Horthy's anti-Communist headquarters were located in Szeged) were the following: striving against Bolshevism, instigating anti-Semitism, and vengeful revisionist positions. The ideological basis for future Hungarian Nazism predated the Italian Fascist movement as well as the formation of Hitler's party.

Horthy's Hungary was obsessed with the destruction of the Jews. It was the first European state to enact anti-Jewish regulations, such as the Numerus Clausus Law, as early as 1920. This Hungarian law limited the access of Jews to higher education by stipulating that the number of Jewish university and high school students had to be proportionate to the percentage of Jews in the overall national population.[9] That legislation violated the League of Nations Treaty on the Protection of Minorities, a multilateral treaty established after World War I as part of the Treaty of Versailles in 1919.

In the 1930s, Gyula Gombosh firmly established a state apparatus that would later ethnically cleanse Hungary. He appointed younger Germanophile chauvinists to state organs and the military.[10] Miklos Horthy approved that process. Meanwhile Horthy, limited by Versailles regulations regarding military power, had been equipping the customs officers, police, and gendarmerie units with regular military equipment.[11]

HUNGARIAN HAND EXTENDED TO THE THIRD REICH

2

CHAPTER

The government of Miklos Horthy was the first European institution to lift the international isolation of the Third Reich.[1] As an alleged token of gratitude, Hitler ceded to Horthy the parts of southern Slovakia which the Hungarian regent occupied in November 1938. In February 1939, Horthy became a member of the Anti-Cominterna bloc. In the spring of the same year, he occupied parts of Trans-Carpathian Ukraine. While gradually moving toward formation of the greater Hungary, Horthy was simultaneously abandoning the League of Nations. In August 1940, northern Transylvania (Erdely) had been given over to his rule.[2]

When granted permission by Hitler to occupy the Trans-Carpathian parts of Ukraine, the Hungarian regent expressed his gratitude to his Führer on March 13, 1939, with these words: "I shall never forget this proof of our friendship, and Your Excellency may certainly always count on my gratitude."[3]

Hungary kept pace with Hitler's successive conquests by adopting ever-increasing anti-Jewish measures—first on May 29, 1938, then in May 1939, and finally on August 2, 1941, when a legislative imitation of Nazi Nuremberg regulations was enforced. Hungarian laws limited the economic activities of Jews, defined them in racial terms, and banned intermarriage.[4]

Miklos Horthy (left) with Adolf Hitler during a conference in Germany in August of 1938.

With his pro-Germanic, pro-Nazi, and revision-oriented supporters, Regent Horthy plotted to take the former Yugoslav Bachka province without a parliamentary decision, most likely in order to avoid discussion in the Hungarian parliament about the Treaty of Friendship signed with Yugoslavia several months prior to the occupation. He accepted Hitler's request to involve the Hungarian army in the dismemberment of Yugoslavia. In return, Hungary would acquire the Banat, Bachka, and Baranya Serbian provinces. On March 30, 1941, in cooperation with Hitler's chief of staff, Horthy's representatives and military headquarters made a plan to deploy Hungarian troops prior to intrusion into Yugoslavia.[5]

In response to Hitler's question posed on the eve of March 27, 1941, regarding validity of the Treaty of Friendship with Yugoslavia, as to whether it meant that Hungary had abandoned territorial aspirations to that country, Horthy wrote on the following day, "The territorial aspirations Your Excellency has alluded to in His message are still an option, waiting for the opportunity to be fully realized."[6]

The extent to which Horthy valued the Treaty of Permanent Peace and Everlasting Friendship Between Hungary and Yugoslavia (ratified on December 12, 1940) may be understood from the fact that prior to the war he actively supported the Ustashi movement by Croatian Roman Catholic Nazis. As soon as the Independent State of Croatia was declared on April 10, 1941, following the invasion of Yugoslavia, the Hungarian government held a session to approve the regent's order for war engagement in "southern regions" and his "Proclamation to the Hungarian People." The proclamation informed the nation about the necessity of military intervention for the sake of protecting the Hungarian population in northern Serbia. On the heels of the formation of an "independent" Roman Catholic Croatia, Horthy proclaimed that the treaty with Yugoslavia was no longer valid, and thus "has emerged our imperative duty to once again take into our hands the destiny and security of the position of Hungarians who live in great numbers in territory that seceded from Hungary in 1918. This is such a sacred national duty that we must carry it out without any further delay."

The regent in his proclamation added a hypocritical note: "My army's actions are not directed against the Serbian nation. We have no objection to that nation and we desire to live in peace with it in the future."[7]

HORTHY'S WAR CRIMES
IN EASTERN EUROPE

3

A royal lieutenant in the Senta Royal Infantry of the Yugoslav army asked the commander of his regiment for permission to halt invading Hungarian occupiers at the village of Sirig. The commander was not interested in resistance, so he left the infantry deployed around Sirig. In a skirmish with the advancing Hungarian army, the infantry destroyed six of the invading tanks. That resistance doomed Sirig.[1]

The last unit of the disarrayed Royal Yugoslav army that marched through Novi Sad was the Third Cavalry regiment from Subotica, a city to the far north, bordering Hungary. Within two days of its retreat, there was no military unit protecting Novi Sad. Local state police maintained some sort of order and turned power over to Hungarian occupation forces when Bachka province and its capital Novi Sad were taken.[2]

APRIL 1941 MASSACRE

Hungarian occupiers marched into Novi Sad with the fixed idea that the city was full of Chetnicks (Serbian resistance forces). On the afternoon of April 13, 1941, the Hungarian military came to Temerinska Street, having received a report from local Hungarians that Chetnicks were supposedly hiding in Salayka, an exclusively Serbian colony in Novi Sad. The occupiers ordered the gates to be opened, removed the local police, searched the houses, and killed residents. At the corner of

Dositeyeva and Almashka streets, where Aleksandra Kolarsky's bakery, called *Sharan* ("Carp"), once stood, there remained a pile of corpses after the Hungarian military had rampaged through the colony. The bakery was completely plundered.[3]

It is estimated that about 700 Serbs were annihilated in the April 1941 pogrom committed by Hungarian troops in Salayka and Podbara, two Novi Sad colonies predominantly populated by Serbs. The number of victims has been deduced from a testimony of Yelka Brzak, a grave digger's daughter, who stated in an interview that all the murdered Serbian civilians were buried at a cemetery called Almashko Groblje. *The Encyclopedia of Military Terminology* states that in April 1941, about 720 individuals—mostly Serbs—were murdered in Novi Sad.[4]

At least 8,350 citizens were murdered during the course of Hungarian occupation of the province of Bachka, due to fake conflicts staged by Hungarian troops for the sake of creating supposed chivalrous battles waged by Horthy's brave forces.[5] In a report dated October 10, 1942, on the political conditions in Bachka province, Svetozar Markovich underlined the fact that by October 1941 some 15,000 individuals had been executed by Horthy's forces, while 60,000 had been evicted and confined to concentration camps. Markovich also wrote that "about 10,000 souls" were executed during a January 1942 Razzia in Shaikashka (a region of south Bachka) and Novi Sad.[6]

VICTIMS OF HORTHY'S INVASION

Hungarian troops received an order to create fake conflicts as if they were engaged in battles with Serbian resistance force, Chetnicks. According to certain references, the April 1941 terror claimed the lives of these civilians:

350 Sirig citizens, 117 Srbobran citizens, 49 Kula citizens, 40 Churug citizens, 484 Senta citizens, 112 Kanyizha citizens, 129 Bachka Topola citizens, 182 Pachir citizens, 21 Haydukovo citizens, and 116 Sombor citizens.[7]

Horthy's army on parade in the spring of 1942 during its occupation of Novi Sad.

Other sources cite different numbers. An unsigned document written in 1942 titled "The Position of Serbs in 'South Hungary,'" records that in April 1941, "about 9,000 massacre victims paid with their lives." On June 11, 1943, a Serbian Secret Service officer wrote from Istanbul to the Royal Yugoslav government-in-exile that Serbian Orthodox communities collected approximate data regarding about 300 victims in Sombor, 123 in Kula, 480 in Srbobran, about 1,500 in Novi Sad, and about 5,000 in Subotica and its vicinity.[8] Milosh Apich, a refugee from Kula, testified to about 136 Serbs murdered in his town.[9]

Based on incomplete data, the Vojvodina Regional Commission for Investigating Crimes Committed by the Occupiers and Their Collaborators determined that the April 1941 occupation of Bachka affected the following colonies:

Ada (17 victims), Aleksa Shantich (8 victims), Baimok (8 victims), Baranya Petrovo Selo (3 victims), Bachko Gradishte (1 victim), Bachki Monoshtor (1 victim), Bachki Petrovac (1 victim), Bachko Petrovo Selo (4 victims), Bachka Topola (70 victims), Beli Manastir (5 victims), Bilye (1 victim), Bodgyani (25 victims), Bolman (6 victims), Branyina (1 victim), Bukin (1 victim), Vayska (2 victims), Bardarac (1 victim), Novi Vrbas (4 victims), Stari Vrbas (1 victim), Gardinovci (1 victim), Darda (3 victims), Deronye (5 victims), Despot Saint Ivan (2 victims), Kovily (2 victims), Gyurgyevo (1 victim), Yagodnyak (3 victims), Kamenatz (1 victim), Karavukovo (2 victims), Kelebiya (4 victims), Knezhevi Vinogradi (1 victim), Kula (49 victims), Lug (2 victims), Mali Igyosh (2 victims), Mol (13 victims), Moshorin (2 victims), Novi Sad (159 victims), Odzhatzy (1 victim), Palich (20 victims), Pachir (16 victims), Pashichevo (1 victim), Petlovatz (2 victims), Plavna (7 victims), Podravlye (1 victim), Popovatz (2 victims), Ridgyitza (6 victims), Rumenka (2 victims), Svetozar Miletich (5 victims), Senta (51 victims), Silbash (1 victim), Sirig (101 victims), Sokolatz (2 victims), Sombor (44 victims), Srbobran (92 victims), Stanishich (7 victims), Stapar (2 victims), Bechey (7 victims), Kanyizha (13 victims), Stara Moravitza (1 victim), Stari Sivatz (2 victims), Stepanovichevo (1 victim), Subotitza (150 victims), Temerin (3 victims), Titel (2 victims), Tovarishevo (1 victim), Toryantzi (1 victim), Feketich (4 victims), Horgosh (21 victims), Tzrvenka (13 victims), Churug (15 victims), and Shaikash (8 victims).[10]

The Commission identified by name altogether 1,015 victims murdered by Horthy's units in April 1941.

Over 10,000 civilians were plundered in the April 1941 occupation. The value of looted property amounted to 539,251,271 pre-war dinars.[11] Such acts represented violations of Articles 46, 47, and 48 of The Hague Convention of 1907.[12] No perpetrator has ever been brought to justice for those violations, nor for numerous other inhumane acts.

The indigenous Serbian community in Hungary proper was not spared from persecutions. Santovo priest Milosh Apich's body was found in a Danube armlet on April 25, 1941. His limbs were all broken. Bullets had been fired at his head. Regional investigators ordered a post-mortem search. The body was later buried in a secret place.[13]

Several hundred Hungarian Serbs were imprisoned, particularly those from intelligence organizations. The Hungarian Ministry of Interior decided to form so-called labor battalions from some of those Serbs and to deport others to concentration camps. The entirety of Jewish intelligence was recruited into "labor battalions." In April 1941, Camp No. 440 was established in Martzal for numerous Serbs in Hungary who were deemed "unworthy of confidence."[14]

One of the most horrible torture prisons in history was situated at the military barracks still standing in Novi Sad. (To this day it is used as military barracks.) The Regional Commission established the names of 412 martyrs who died in the course of brutal tortures and investigations that were carried out in Horthy's prison.[15]

Horthy personally authorized the chief of staff to establish courts martial. The order to establish such courts called upon Nazi laws and regulations. Sometime during the first two months of the occupation, the British newspaper *The Times* published an article stating that, "Hungarians are competing with Germans and Bulgarians on who shall commit greater atrocities against the Serbs." [16] The decision to establish courts martial in order to process actions against the Hungarian state (crimes of treason, uprising and associations to commit such acts) was announced by Bela Novakovich, the South Army department commander.[17]

On October 28, 1941, the Hungarian government declared that the chief of staff was the sole person in charge of instigating court-martials for soldiers and civilians accused of treason. The criminal charges for grand treason were defined in terms of actions that would "inflict harm to Hungarian military and its allies' militaries, or contribute to military efforts of the enemy."[18] It is very certain as to which militaries were considered by Horthy and his colleagues as allies. Horthy's chief of staff was rehabilitated at the beginning of this century.

Sixty-four anti-Fascists had been hung and shot, while around 900 had been imprisoned by the end of 1941.[19] Up to October 1, 1942, 350 Communist party members had been hung, shot, and murdered during police investigations and detained in Hungarian dungeons, while over 5,000 resistance movement sympathizers had been languishing in prisons and camps.[20]

The Hungarian regent violated international law (The Hague Convention, Article 23) when he forcefully conscripted youth in the occupied areas. That act was also a violation of Article 42 which forbids usurpations of foreign sovereignty during occupations.[21]

In spite of the fact that during its session held on December 16, 1941, the Hungarian parliament had unanimously declared occupied Bachka and other occupied former Yugoslav lands as territories annexed to their motherland. Acting in a capacity of a sovereign state in those regions commenced in July 1941, right after military administration was declared in those areas. Later, the administration was handed over to civil authorities. In the same month, the male youth born in the 1920–1922 period, as well as secondary school students born in the 1915–1919 period, were called up into the Hungarian army.[22]

Confidential orders regarding recruitment of Serbs and Jews into labor and military units had been issued throughout the war. One of those was the Order of Hungarian Minister of Interior 13400/VII.1942; then the Order of Bachka Vice Chief 348/1942; as well as orders by local command of the Hungarian military organization Leventa in Bachka Topola No. 11 and 83/1943; also the Fifth Szeged Corps orders 14489/sub.IV.1944 and 22087/1944; and the Order of Minister of Interior 11135/VII 1944. Upon such orders, in May 1942, Serbian officers in reserve and some active officers of the former Royal Yugoslav army were called up for retraining.

A recruitment of the Slavic-origin population in particular was implemented in October 1942. Call-ups to military and supposed labor service were also sent in February, March, June, September, and October 1943, as well as in January, May, June, August, and September 1944.[23]

Medical personnel in mobilization centers located in Sombor, Subotica, Novi Vrbas, Szeged and Budapest declared all Serbian men capable of military service. They were assigned to various military capacities—except aviation—either in units composed solely of

Slavic-origin soldiers or in Hungarian units. Mobilized Serbs, Slavs, and Jews had no leave, nor permission to leave their military barracks. Their food was of very poor quality and punishments were harsher. They had no rest from heavy physical labor. Some Hungarian soldiers purposefully boasted before the Serbian soldiers of how they had murdered many Serbian civilians in the January 1942 Razzia. Those soldiers who reacted to such provocations were court-martialed and condemned to beatings, prisons, and gallows.[24]

Forcefully recruited soldiers were punished if they engaged in conversation with locals, bought food, sought medical help, or reported Hungarian crimes in occupied territories to the east (Ukraine and Russia). Sometimes their guilt was simply fabricated. When individual soldiers deserted from the Hungarian army and fled to the Red Army and partisan units, the remaining conscripted Serbs, Jews, and Slavs were massacred en masse because they were considered hostages by the Hungarian Nazi forces.[25]

Mobilized Serbs were also condemned to punitive battalions or sent to the most dangerous points on the Eastern Front. Hungarian officers often stated aloud that Serbs and Slavs were "good only to receive Red Army bullets."[26] According to one witness, mobilized ethnic Bachka Hungarians were placed in the first front line, ahead of other Hungarian soldiers.[27]

VICTIMS OF THE FIFTH SZEGED CORPS

By order of the Fifth Szeged Corps, on May 1, 1944, Bachka men aged forty-five to sixty-two were called up to 142 mobilization centers in Subotica and 145 in Sombor. Many of the 4,400 called-up men suffered from heart problems and other maladies. The medical committee had declared even the maimed and deaf as capable of military service.

Three weeks after recruitment training, they were sent to Austria where many became ill. Gravely ill soldiers were dismissed, while those in good health were deployed among the occupation armies in Austria and France. A Serbian contingent was sent to the Italian front where many were killed in combat. Those who were totally unfit for military service were sent to hard labor.

The above-mentioned corps had also conscripted the Serbian and Slavic youth, aged seventeen to twenty, in June 1944. Hungarian Nazi military and gendarmerie collected Serbian youth from Bachka villages and placed them under the command of the 17th German Aviation Division. That Nazi division deployed Serbian youth to Austrian and German airports and forced them to repair damages, remove stones, and clear ruins. The youth were often forced to work amidst bombings from the Western allies.

Serbian youth and elderly "recruits" were pressured to join SS units. Many refused, some paying with their lives. The National Commission for Investigation of the Crimes of Occupiers and their Collaborators found that "the overwhelming majority" of the forcefully recruited Serbs who were transported to Germany and Austria never returned home.[28]

SERBS KILLED ON THE EASTERN FRONT

The National Commission was not able to determine a precise number of Serbian soldiers sacrificed by the Hungarian Nazis on the Eastern Front. However, it is estimated that a huge percentage of those were killed. Hungarian and German troops monitored from behind the lines of conscripted Serbian soldiers and shot anyone suspected of attempting to escape. The commission quoted Dushan Lukich of Stapar, who said that in his unit 100 out of 120 Serbs were murdered in this fashion. The commission commented upon his statement, saying "that in the same manner thousands upon thousands of forcefully conscripted soldiers were killed."[29]

Szeged prison Chilag (or "Star") was the largest political prison in Great Hungary. It was a jail for resistance movement members who resisted as Communists, Communist youth, and sympathizers. In that dungeon, 752 prisoners from Bachka and Baranya served their sentences. Four were executed in the very prison (Grozda Gayishin, Erne

Kish, Pavle Kardelis, and Aleksandar Popov-Zhivkov), while 334 other inmates were sent to forced labor (sixty-five survived the war). Toward the end of the war, 100 prisoners were sent to German Nazi death camps (twenty-six survived). More than 425 Chilag inmates lost their lives in the winds of war.[30]

A certain number of Chilag prisoners were sent to the Eastern Front on October 13, 1942, as Troop No. 451. Of that troop, 45 Bachka resistance movement members of Hungarian, Serbian, Slovak, Ruthenian and Jewish origin (including an ethnic German, Gabriel Nachtingale) were killed.[31] Other members of the resistance movement were sent to the Eastern Front on November 20, 1942, as Troop No. 452. It was composed of Bachka ethnic Serbs, Croats, Ruthenians, Slovaks, Hungarians, a Jew, Philip Stein, and an Italian, Martin Augustin.[32] The third group of resistance movement members against Hungarian Nazism was sent to the Eastern Front on November 20, 1942, within Troop No. 453. Of that troop, 150 members were killed: Bachka ethnic Serbs, Hungarians, Jews, Ruthenians, Slovaks, Croats, and a German, Nikola Shlarp.[33]

Miklos Horthy was responsible for those 333 martyrs that were sent to certain death. Of those 333 victims, 246 were ethnic Serbs, 24 Ruthenians, 19 Hungarians, 18 Slovaks, 17 Jews, 3 Croats, 2 Germans, 1 Italian, 1 Ukrainian, and 1 Czech. Seven citizens of Churug also lost their lives during their prison terms in Chilag.[34]

MASSACRE AT KOMARNO

During the Hungarian army's retreat before the invading Red Army, Horthy's soldiers and commanders murdered "a large number of Serbs" at Komarno when they refused to continue retreating with the army they were forced to join.

Several individuals survived that organized murder. After the war they suffered from chronic health problems, which they incurred from hunger, forced marches, wounds, lack of medical attention, and inhumane treatment.[35]

FORCED LABOR

The National Commission established that at least 21,671 individuals from territories occupied by Horthy were sent to forced labor. The highest Hungarian authorities issued confidential orders that civilians be recruited for forced labor in order to contribute to war invasions and for the sake of the destruction of Serbian, Jewish, and Slavic ethnicities. The most significant confidential genocidal orders came from the minister of interior, Ferentz Kerestesh Fischer (filed under No. 13400/VII 1942) and the Bachka county vice president (filed under No. 150/142).[36]

Immediately following the occupation of Bachka, in accordance with Horthy's anti-Semitic policies, Jews aged eighteen to forty-eight were forcefully recruited to build roads and warehouses and work on the land allotted to Hungarian settlers. The initial labor forces were composed exclusively of Jews, by order of the Pechuy division commander, General Terek. At the end of April 1941, Terek ordered that forty Jews from Sombor be sent to Gakovo to clean trenches and remove tank obstacles. In May, about 400 Jews built the road Stapar-Bachki Brestovatz, while being exposed to the cruelties of Hungarian Honveds (soldiers).[37] Within a short time, Serbs and individuals of Slavic origin were added to the Jewish labor forces.

Forced laborers were also sent to Hungary, Ukraine, Belarus, Czechoslovakia, Austria, Germany, Romania, and parts of the former Yugoslavia to serve as reinforcements to occupation forces. They were forced to install barbed wire, clear minefields along the front lines, build bunkers and fortifications, load war materiel, install telephone lines in the line of fire, build military airports, cut forests, build railways, perform slave labor in mines, factories and shipyards, clear ruins, and till the ground.

Hungarian occupiers particularly used the Serbs from south Bachka, the area called Shaikashka, to clear minefields.

South Bachka (Shaikashka) had the highest concentration of Serbs per capita. Shaikashka had always been a source of irritation for Hungarians because it enjoyed a broad autonomy granted by the Viennese court in the former Austro-Hungarian Empire. It was in Shaikashka that Horthy's troops carried out ethnic cleansing in January 1942.

In a very short time, 25 percent of the forcefully mobilized craftsmen from Shaikashka lost their lives in the no-man's-land between the two opposing armies. Only eight out of 108 political prisoners, Serbs and Jews, remained.

Conditions for the forced laborers were cruel, like those imposed by the Nazis. Many froze to death due to temperatures that reached 40 degrees below zero (Centigrade). Daily labor would last for twelve hours. However, "working hours" were often extended to twenty. Carrying loads that weighed 1,800-2,000 kilograms was a daily norm for the crews of ten to fifteen slave workers assigned to railway construction. Those who were unable to sustain such loads experienced merciless punishments.

Serbs also shed their blood in the Varpalota coal mine where they had to dig for twelve hours incessantly, without meals—food was given to them after "working hours." Workshop slave laborers were hit in the face, beaten with pickaxes and rods, and hung.

In early spring, some forced laborers worked in rice fields the whole day long, even on Sundays and national holidays. They became ill from the cold water, and had bruised arms and legs from retrieving barbed wire from 80-meter-deep water. There were no clean clothes, footwear, medical examinations, or medicine for the Serbs and Jews. Winds blew through barracks that were always wet with rain. Lighting a fire to get dry or warm was not permitted. They had no blankets.

The cold and damp claimed many lives of our kin in the extensive areas of the East. There are many unmarked graves in the East. They are not even mentioned in Serbian national history. When those slave soldiers were transported in cattle cars, they did not receive food for ten days. They were later "fed" with soups made from dry turnips and cabbage leaves. Daily bread portions were reduced from 200 to 100 grams. Those who worked in agricultural fields were fed with meat from decayed cattle.

Unloading war materials and building fortifications continued day and night under all weather conditions. Enslaved Serbs and Jews were shackled, thrown in dark pits filled with mud and water, beaten, and tortured to death. A special method of torture was to hang a person so that only the toes touched the ground. When the "punished" passed out from pain, the perpetrators would pour cold water over the victim to continue the torment repeatedly. Another method of "punishment" was to tie a prisoner in a hank-like form and put sticks between his knees.[38]

Sadistic cruelties at Bor mine in central Serbia, where a contingent of Bachka Jews were sent for forced labor for the German Nazi interests, were expressions of the darkest depths of human nature. The slave laborers from Bachka were monitored by the Hungarian soldiers. Death sentences were a daily occurrence. As the liberation army advanced toward Serbia, many Bor slave laborers were forced to retreat northward with the Hungarian occupation troops. When they reached Crvenka, in Bachka, 1,000 were shot.[39]

More than 1,800 individuals were taken for slave labor from the Shaikashka settlements of Zhabaly, Churug, Gyurdgevo, and Gospodyinci. The Hungarian Nazis brutally murdered at least eleven Zhabaly residents, thirty-six Churug residents, ten Gyurgyevo residents, and eight Gospodyinci residents.[40]

Besides forced labor, Horthy's anti-Semitic and anti-Serbian authorities enacted other regulations that applied to those particularly hated ethnic groups. In April 1941, the Hungarian army command (citing Order 4) prohibited Jews in the surrounding regions from entering areas occupied by Hungary. On September 19 of the same year, the ministry of military issued an order forbidding admission of Jews into the regular army, in favor of auxiliary ("labor") units. On November 20, 1942, the order was extended as the consequence of an amendment to the law of national defense. The amendment stipulated that Serbs and Jews, being "a lower race and unreliable individuals," may not serve even as part of auxiliary units, but males age twenty-one to forty-eight were to be included into "labor service."[41]

EXPULSION OF NON-HUNGARIAN POPULATION

According to certain Hungarian data, after the end of World War I in 1918, 2,675 volunteer settlers had migrated to Bachka, as well as 373 Chetnicks, 1,072 Slovenians, 36 Romanians, 186 Bulgarians, 35 Albanians, 195 Czechs and Slovaks, 1,425 Russians, and 851 of other unspecified ethnicities.[42]

The Hungarian news agency reported from the Bachka town of Subotica that by April 30, 1941, over 10,000 people had been deported and at least 100,000 more Serbs remained for expulsion. The Hungarian government contacted the German occupation authorities in Belgrade (the capital of Serbia) to seek permission to expel at least 150,000 Serbs from Hungary to central Serbia. That means that besides the Bachka Serbian population, the entire native Serbian population in Hungary proper was destined for expulsion. German Nazi authorities refused the plan because of potential economic difficulties for central Serbia and the influx of potential resistance fighters. [43]

About 1,500 Bunyevatz ethnic members were expelled from the village of Rata (in the municipality of Subotica) by authority of the self-styled "Patron of Bunyevatz people." The Hungarian forces murdered several dozen Bunyevatz community members.[44]

When German Nazis prohibited further expulsions to central Serbia, Hungarian authorities began ridding the occupied territory of Serbian people at night before the German authorities could comprehend what was underway and prevented further deportations. At that point, Horthy's death machinery reached a secret agreement with another Hitler satellite—the Independent State of Croatia—about "acceptance" of unwanted Serbs and Jews. Prior to the breakup of Yugoslavia, the Croatian Roman Catholic Nazis (the Ustashi) were sheltered in Horthy's Hungary. Thus, the Ustashi authorities in the Vatican-created, World War II-era Croatian state favorably responded to the request of their ideological patron. Numerous Serbs and Jews were liquidated as soon as Hungarians exported them across the rivers Drava and Danube (on the frontier between Hungary and Croatia). Other expelled Serbs and Jews were confined to the Ustashi's

Jasenovac death camp (the most gruesome death camp of World War II). By the end of May 1941, 42,000 Serbs and an unknown number of Jews were expelled to the Croatian slaughterhouse.[45] They fell as victims in the death factory that was created and sustained by the Independent State of Croatia, under the blessings from the Vatican.

POPULATING BACHKA WITH ETHNIC HUNGARIANS

On March 20, 1941, the presidency of Horthy's government made an official study on deportations, evictions, returns, and population exchanges. Croats from the Medymurye region and the Baranya triangle were scheduled for exchange, while Zala Croats and the Shokatz community were scheduled for expulsion. Accomplices to that crime were various publications, associations, and institutions.

In April 1941, the Hungarian National Association of Engineers and Constructors wrote a memorandum about the Slavic populace expulsion. The memorandum text states:

> *Orthodox Serbian population will always be a body within the body that infests the entire organism. Only a radical cutting out of that body can bring about true healing. The Bunyevatz community should be included in the same measures because they are not loyal to Hungary, thus they should be—along with other unwanted individuals—expelled across Danube and Drava. Get them out!* [46]

On April 25, 1941, a top confidential order, 1477/41, was issued. It instructed the Hungarian police, gendarmerie, and, if necessary, military troops to arrest the most dangerous elements (Slavic and Jewish elements), as well as other enemies of the Hungarian state in "the southern region." Confinement was ordered for all individuals who were not native to Bachka, those who did not recognize the new order and instigated unrest, members of the Chetnick organization, leaders of volunteer settlers, and optants (those who migrated to Yugoslavia after new borders were drawn between Yugoslavia and Hungary following World

War I). Hungarian state organs were also ordered to arrest opponents of Hungary. In the interest of hastening the genocide, Horthy's authorities issued an additional order on April 27, 1941: post-World War I settlements of veterans, as well as settlements of others who had populated Bachka for agricultural reasons following the war, were to be deported within three days starting at midnight on April 28.[47]

Preserved documents contain information that Horthy's institutions seriously considered evicting the entire native Bachka population that fell under the "Slavic elements" determinant, with the explanation that their involvement in war against the Austro-Hungarian Empire proved they were not loyal to the Hungarian state and thus should be punished.[48]

On April 17, Stara Kanyizha lost 150 residents to eviction. Beginning on April 15, eighty-eight Martonosh settlers experienced the terror.

On April 21, 1941, all of the settlers from the Stepanovichevo colony were evicted. The criminals threw an old woman, incapable of walking further, overboard into the Danube from a ferry boat at Begech. Sirig villagers who were not exterminated on April 13 (when about 450 out of 1,450 settlers were killed) were incarcerated in concentration camps. Among the villagers of Staro Gyurgyevo, 873 were evicted to Srem (an area occupied by the Croatian Nazi Ustasha state), where the SS and Ustashi troops immediately slaughtered forty-six. From Alpar-Vayska, 255 villagers were evicted, while 200 residents from surrounding villages were deported to Nazi Croatia.

On April 13, 1,400 Baymochka Rata citizens were evicted to Barch concentration camp for Serbs.

Approximately 500 residents of Veternik were systematically expelled beginning on April 21. On the same day, 90 Voyvoda Mishich residents were deported, and the remaining 160 citizens were expelled from their homes a month later. Those expelled lived in Old Futog colony, in stables and sheds. Additionally, 90 inhabitants of Novi Kisach were deported, as well as Tankosichevo residents (180 were evicted overnight along with residents from other colonies). Genocidal perpetrators evicted 300 Mol citizens from their homes and with cruel treatment marched them to the Danube to be deported.

Native ethnic Hungarians tormented 123 Voyvoda Zimovich villagers in April 1941 before deporting them on April 22 (Croatian Ustashi murdered six of those residents in Herzegovina). Also in the month of April, 1,751 Senta residents were systematically evicted (sixty-seven World War I veterans who had settled there were murdered in the very town).

On April 22, 354 Kovily village residents were expelled to Croatia-occupied province of Srem. Bodyanski Rit lost 150 settlers to eviction (thirteen of whom were murdered by Croatian Ustashi while passing through Croatia). From Tomichevo, 500 residents were deported to Vatican-created Nazi Croatia.

On April 23, Horthy's anti-Semites evicted fourteen Jewish families from Temerin. They later returned to their homes only to be exterminated during the January 1942 massacre. The Hungarian Nazis deported 300 Lok village residents. Among the residents of Bachko Petrovo Selo, 258 were evicted. About 200 Gardinovci villagers were deported to Srem. On April 25, 121 Shaikash villagers were also evicted to Srem, the province occupied by the Nazi Independent State of Croatia.

During April and May, sixty-seven individuals from Katch were deported.

On May 8, 103 Tzrvenka citizens were evicted (forty-seven fled just prior to invasion). During that crime, the occupiers crushed the jaw of one victim with an iron rod and three ribs of another. On the same day, 1,340 Sokolatz residents were evicted: 994 were expelled to central Serbia, 92 were jailed, 213 were deported to Sharvar concentration camp for Serbs, and many more were evicted to Srem, Banat, Dalmatia, and Herzegovina. Of the villagers at Novo Selo Feketich, 245 were evicted.

On May 19, 300 Tomislavtzi residents were forced by gendarmerie to Novi Sad. When the Hungarian occupiers did not manage to expel them to the Vatican-created Croatian Nazi state, a month later they were deported to Sharvar concentration camp for Serbs. On June 12, they were sent to Sharvar, where 100 died. From Srednyi Salash, 245 residents were evicted (twenty-four died in death camps).

On May 28, 1,500 Hadzitchevo villagers were forced to sign volunteer renouncements of their property prior to being expelled from their homes. Those who refused were either jailed or sent to a concentration camp. All Milesheva residents—420 people—were expelled on May 29.

In June, 500 Moshorin residents were sent to Belgrade on a barge. On June 4, 905 Radivoyevichevo residents were expelled. All 700 residents of Gornya Rogatitza were deported. At least 235 Karkatur village residents were expelled. The occupiers declared 113 of them "bandits."

Beginning in 1943, 318 Horgosh residents were gradually and systematically exterminated. They were forced out of their homes, left to roam in the streets, beg, and attempt to survive. Meanwhile, the "Rondyosh guard" made sure to torment and murder those homeless Serbs.

All 1,400 Vasilyevichevo villagers were expelled by systematic terror starting on May 6. All 96 Mala Gyala villagers were forced out of their homes and remained in the streets until the winter of 1943, when they were deported to Sharvar concentration camp for Serbs.

At Velebit, 904 villagers were evicted, and at Uzunovichevo 156 residents were also expelled.

At Gornyi Breg, 63 villagers were evicted, and 550 Bachko Dushanovo residents were deported to Sharvar camp on May 23. Among the victims of expulsion were 384 Svetichevo settlers, along with 179 Nyegoshevo residents.

From Haydukovo, 516 residents were also expelled.

Among the citizens of Masarikovo, 154 were deported to Sharvar camp for Serbs, where eleven died because the occupiers did not manage to evict them to Ustasha Nazi Croatia. Among the victims of expulsion were also 31 Naumovichevo residents, as well as 320 Mali Beograd residents.

In May, 170 Kotchitchevo villagers were deported to Sharvar. Only twelve returned after the war. Of the 1,600 Karagyordgyevo residents deported to Sharvar, 151 died and fourteen were shot at that concentration camp for Serbs.

On June 13, 460 Mishichevo residents were deported to Barch concentration camp for Serbs. From Sombor, fourteen families were deported.

On June 14, 500 Aleksa Shantich villagers were deported, fourteen of them to Barch.

On June 17, 120 Bunyevatz community members were evicted just before Chango Hungarians moved into their homes; the evicted were made to paint their own homes prior to abandoning them.

Based on the above data, it is obvious that altogether 25,596 individuals were affected by the expulsions that were rooted in Horthy's political work and orders.[49]

Hungarians who were aided by the occupation forces settled the homes of murdered, evicted, imprisoned, and drafted citizens. New Hungarian settlers exploited mostly the local Serbian population. The new settlers belonged to an ethnic group called the "Chango." Researcher Danilo Uroshevich explains that the origin of this name has not been resolved. Following Hungarian migration led by Arpad, Chango Hungarians remained in Bukovina, Moldavia, and the vicinity of the Romanian town Brasho, separated from their motherland. During the seventeenth and eighteenth centuries, many of the Changos were moved to Serbian-populated military areas.

Since they were close to Romanians and, to a certain extent, the Roma population, Chango Hungarians mingled with those ethnic groups, absorbed much of the Romanian influence, and formed a specific dialect. In the nineteenth century, the rescue of Chango Hungarians began when they were moved to Transylvania. At the beginning of the last century, the Hungarian government commissioner worked on relocating the Changos. Following Horthy's occupation of Transylvania, parts of Slovakia, Baranya, and Bachka, the Hungarian government appointed Jozheph Antal to expel the local populations and settle the Changos. Evicted Bachka residents who were not expelled to central Serbia or the Independent State of Croatia were deported to Hungarian camps for Serbs.[50]

May 1941 marked the beginning of settling Sekely Hungarians from Bukovina, Changos from Moldavia, and Hungarians from Bosnia into Bachka. In July, 1941, 2,500 Hungarian individuals moved from the Serbian capital of Belgrade to the Bachka administrative center at Novi

Sad.[51] In the next two years, 19,385 Hungarians were moved to ethnically cleansed Bachka and Baranya Serbian territories.[52] Those settlers fled en masse before the advancing Red Army and moved into homes abandoned by ethnic Germans from southern Hungarian municipalities. The majority of Chango Hungarians fled to Tolna municipality (capital Seksard).[53]

ETHNOCIDE

Horthy's regime banned newspapers in the Serbian, Slovakian, and Ruthenian languages, as well as sixteen newspapers in Hungarian. None of the forty-seven publications in the German language was outlawed.

The Slovakian secondary school in Bachki Petrovatz was closed. Jews were forbidden access to public services. They were excluded even from physical fitness clubs. Every trace of Yugoslavia and Serbia was removed. Names of settlements and streets were changed to Hungarian. The official books were kept only in Hungarian. The process to Hungarianize names was underway. Former Austro-Hungarian municipalities were set up again as a sign of the "restored integrity" of Saint Stephen's Hungary.[54]

During the April 1941 occupation, Horthy's criminals plundered the famous Serbian monastery of Kovily. Icons, the silver-encrusted monastery charter, and numerous books were stolen from the monastery library.[55]

Serbs were drafted forcefully into the Hungarian army, under threat of death, and had to swear loyalty oaths to Horthy and Hitler (in violation of the Hague Convention, Article 45). They were also forced to sing Hungarian songs and learn Hungarian since they were forbidden to speak their Serbian "dog language."[56]

In the concentration camp at Bachka Topola, prisoners were forced to act like horses by pulling carts and other devices around, in four-hour-long shifts. They were beaten and whipped to the point of fainting, were stripped naked in front of everyone, battered, and called "stinky Serbs" and "bandits." Many were admonished to Hungarianize their names and convert to Roman Catholicism. Those who refused were imprisoned or forced to labor under the worst possible conditions.[57]

HORTHY'S DEATH CAMPS FOR SERBS

On December 16, 1941, the Hungarian parliament declared Bachka and other annexed occupied territories as integral parts of the Hungarian state. On that occasion, Hungarian Prime Minister Laslo Bardoshy greeted "members of the Bunyevatz and Shokatz communities who have always been faithful people in the Megymurye region, as well as the Serbs who have now returned, having known all the time where they belonged."[58] The Nazi Hungarian state formed fifteen camps for prisoners of war and forty for the civilian population.[59]

Early on the morning of June 4, 1941, Hungarian gendarmerie and military troops closed the roads around Novi Zhednik. With guns pointed, they stormed into Serbian houses and drove the families out. The residents were loaded onto trucks and driven to a transitory camp, Radanovatz, where numerous Jews from the Subotica municipality were incarcerated. Three out of 220 Novi Zhednik prisoners died from camp conditions—a two-month-old baby and two adults. Males older than fourteen were driven to Apatin, but the largest number of Novi Zhednik citizens ended up in Barch concentration camp for Serbs.[60]

Danilo Uroshevich testifies that on June 14, 1941, Hungarian military and gendarmerie with feathers (elite troops within the Hungarian gendarmerie serving as public security) occupied Baimok around 11 a.m. They drove the families of the World War I veterans and optants to the schoolyard. After calling them out by name, the occupiers drove them to the railway station. Local Bunyevatz community members, as well as ethnic Hungarians and Germans, shoved bread, soap, and other small items to Serbian families, the large number of Bunyevatz community members, and several poor Hungarian families, who were then loaded into cattle cars. Their homes were given over to Chango Hungarians.

The Hungarian authorities told the deported they were being returned to the areas of origin they had left after World War I. However, at Sombor juncture the Serbs from the Rastina and Aleksa Shantich colonies were loaded onto cars as well. At Baya railway station the deportation was halted for several hours, enabling the locals to supply some prisoners with water. Late at night on June 15, 1941, the deported arrived at Camp Barch. The prisoners were searched, and spoons, forks, knives, scissors, razors, and similar items were confiscated.[61]

When the first inmates arrived on June 15, 1941, Camp Barch in Hungary had been founded 14 kilometers away from the Croatian town of Virovitica. The camp consisted of a seven-floor mill house and "bachelor room" where the single men were heavily guarded. Soon, the citizens of Mali Beograd, Karkature, Karagyorgyevo, Radivoyevichevo, Novi Zhednik, Rogatitza, and Haydukovo, who up to that point had been detained in Apatin camp, were deported to Barch camp for Serbs.[62]

Each family was granted a few square meters of bare floor. They had to drink water from the river Drava at the spot where sewage from improvised toilets flowed. It is painful to describe the merciless treatment that prisoners received from the camp commander, guards, and most soldiers.

During "food distribution" (food consisted of turnip pottage or potato soup and was worse than waste for pigs) the guards assaulted women with children, old women, and women in general; they took them out of the line, and beat them until they fell to the ground or attempted to run away. Single men were beaten and humiliated at every turn, even for the smallest things. Hunger was unbearable. The first victims died within a month.

The political work of Miklos Horthy signed more than 1,200 children, aged three to six, over to the Barch concentration camp for Serbs. All the children aged three and younger starved and died in misery. Older children wriggled under barbed wire and roamed the kitchen waste area, searching for crusts of bread and potato peelings. Maladies took lives every single day. Corpses of the elderly and infants were transported by horse carts and then buried outside the municipal cemetery.[63]

After several weeks, the camp administration selected younger males and females for work in the surrounding heaths. Well-meaning locals supplied prisoners with food staples, sometimes even with medicine. Particular suppliers were Croats from the villages of Potonye, Lukovishche, Brlabash, and Novo Selo. They worked in a heath in the vicinity of Potonye. On several occasions, they drove carts loaded with food into the camp.

Due to the efforts of some prisoners' relatives and friends in Serbia, 198 prisoners were boarded on a train for Belgrade. When the train stopped in Pechuy for five hours, the local Serbs, Shokatz community members, and other citizens cordially brought out food, water, and medicine.

The grave sites of the Serbs who died at the Hungarian concentration camp, Sharvar.

Camp Barch for Serbs was closed at the beginning of December. More than 1,300 prisoners were first deported to Nadykanyizha camp, and then to Sharvar camp.[64]

Following the collapse of Poland, a large number of Polish soldiers fled to Hungary, the country that had traditionally maintained good relations with Poland. Certain soldiers were accommodated in a former silk factory at Sharvar. As Polish soldiers gradually left the site, the camp was emptied in the end.

The first group of Serbian prisoners of war arrived on April 12, 1941. Sharvar was the largest prisoner-of-war camp among the camps in Baja, Ersekujvar, Petervashar, and Komarom. According to Hungarian sources, on April 26, 1941, the camp established by Horthy contained nine officers and 246 soldiers. By May 20, there were about 4,000 prisoners of war. Besides Serbs, the prisoners were of Macedonian, Croatian, Bunyevatz, Slovenian, and Albanian descent.[65]

On May 29, 1941, Sharvar was no longer a prisoner of war camp. It was turned into a torment ground for the Serbian population that had colonized Bachka (after World War I). The ministry of interior, in collaboration with the ministry of military, decided to speedily detain up to 15,000 Serbs because Chango Hungarians had arrived ahead of schedule. Dwellers from twenty-five exclusively Serbian settlements were crammed into the crowded Novi Sad concentration camp "Aerodrome" and later transported by cattle cars to Sharvar camp. The first prisoners arrived at that scaffold of the Serbian people on June 13, 1941. According to Hungarian sources, on June 27, 1941, 3,898 Serbs were detained in Sharvar camp.[66]

During the course of 1941 and 1942, 1,500 mothers were confined to Sharvar camp, along with 4,500 children, several hundred children under three, numerous babies, and the elderly.[67] The camp claimed 400 lives in the first five months of its operation.[68]

In the beginning of 1942, when the genocidal Razzia was organized, the majority of Sharvar camp prisoners were colonized Bachka and Baranya villagers, numerous Slovenians from the occupied Slovenian town Lendava and its surroundings, and Gradishte Croats considered "unreliable" from Hungarian point of view.[69]

In 1942, 200 Medgymurye Slovenians had been deported to Sharvar camp. Altogether, 650 Slovenians become Sharvar prisoners.[70]

In June 1941, incoming Sharvar inmates found the remaining Polish refugees. Namely, three Polish medics remained out of Slavic solidarity upon learning that the former silk factory was to be turned into a concentration camp for Serbs. As much as Sharvar was a forbidden topic in the Serbian textbooks, so were the righteous Poles who have no testimonial account in Serbian history. Their names were Stanislav Tsarzhensky, Bozhenevsky, and Tadeus Vohl. Doctor Tsarzhensky, particularly remembered for his kindness to the inmates, managed to escape and become a physician to the Sixth Liberation Army Corps.[71]

Serbian inmates were detained in nine factory workshops. Located at the center of that tomb—officially named "The Hungarian Royal Camp"—were the camp administration, kitchen, and dwellings for guards and soldiers. Some light managed to penetrate into the camp through the concrete roof.

Wooden beds stacked three high—real mews—got crowded. Each inmate was allotted forty centimeters of space. Countless insects and lice infested the barracks. There was no protection from rain. In winter the straw scattered on the floor and beds got wet and rotted.

These conditions, along with terrible nutrition—turnips and rotten waste from Hungarian warehouses—contributed to a tuberculosis epidemic. By order of the Hungarian Ministry of Interior on June 27, 1941, the already miserable food portions were further limited to "ten dekagrams of sugar per week" and "four monthly kilograms of flour per head."[72]

The Hungarian military and gendarmerie whipped and beat the prisoners with batons for no reason. Danilo Uroshevich remembers camp commanders as mostly cruel and "often bloodthirsty—worse than a beast." They whipped inmates over the most sensitive body parts.

Whoever resisted the camp regime was confined to "Star," a building with iron doors and a star-like window. Space in Star allowed prisoners to sit only or to stand. The castigated were allotted 100 grams of bread and a portion of water daily. Typhoid, bloody dysentery, and tuberculosis were rampant. Because of non-existent hygiene, pregnant women in filthy barracks often lost their lives during childbirth. In 1941-1942, 146 newborn babies died. Horthy's policies doomed thousands of Serbian children to a gradual death.[73]

Corpses from the Sharvar scaffold were often buried in groups of four, and entire families were thrown into biers. Only the closest relatives were allowed to accompany the dead to the cemetery, yet many were buried in secret. They were often thrown into unmarked pits near the cemetery.[74] There was no mention in Serbian history classes of the uncanny crimes committed under Horthy.

Researcher and witness to crimes Danilo Uroshevich writes that the most gruesome conditions in Sharvar camp for Serbs came to be in the winter of 1941-1942. Starving children assailed food carts in an effort to snatch potatoes, and were not deterred even by whipping. In the waste enclosure, children collected potato peelings and baked them. They also searched for stale bread morsels to cook in water.

Certain Sharvar locals practiced smuggling food over barbed wire, even though access to the wire was strictly forbidden to both children and locals. The locals passed bread, bacon, and fruit to children. A few of the more humane guards tolerated such locals, knowing that Serbian children were starving to death.[75] The highest death rate at the camp occurred in the spring of 1942.[76]

Families were driven by guards to bathe together. For cultures with no family custom of bathing together naked, this was yet another forced humiliation.

Inmates "employed" outside the camp brought in food primarily to ill children. These workers, who were lucky enough to work at private properties, in most cases had tolerable accommodations and food because Hungarian peasants appreciated their labor and supplied them with necessities.

The Serbian Orthodox Church in Hungary and Bachka engaged in a rescue of Sharvar camp children and families. By October 1944, the Hospital of Serbian Orthodox communities in Bachka parish had admitted 450 camp children ill with tuberculosis.[77]

Praiseworthy individuals also rescued some victims from the Sharvar ordeal. Antal Kish was an outstanding example in his rescuing mission. Throughout the occupation of Novi Zhednik, he rescued several generations of his fellow citizens to whom he had no obligation whatsoever. Words of comfort to prisoners in Nagy Kanyizha and Sharvar camps were provided by "the mother of inmates" Yagitza Mutzakova, an old lady from Subotica who customarily brought food staples and clothing to the suffering Serbs.[78]

Gyergy Tashnadi, nicknamed "Beardy," was a typical example of an executor of Horthy's policies. He covered up his cruelty to camp inmates whenever Orthodox Church delegations and similar committees visited the camp. On such occasions the refinement, politeness, compliance, and good will of that criminal were on full display. Only then did starved inmates get better treatment, more plentiful and better food.[79]

A Barch camp survivor recalls that victims buried outside the municipal cemetery were not placed in caskets, and neither were their resting places marked. Thus, in the case of at least "several hundred deceased inmates" it is unknown where their remains are buried.

Uroshevich further writes that a "countless number of crosses at Sharvar cemetery, as well as countless unmarked graves outside the cemetery," also represent a testimony to the suffering of Sharvar inmates. He claims that more than 1,000 individuals succumbed to tuberculosis—mostly children and the elderly. Each family lost at least one member, while many lost all their offspring. Some families completely died out.

Out of 450 children admitted by October 1944 to the Hospital of Serbian Orthodox communities in Bachka parish, forty died.[80]

HORTHY'S GENOCIDE IN ROMANIA

Frightening crimes against civilians, similar to those of the Razzia, were committed against Romanians and Jews in occupied Transylvania. Those ethnic groups were initially targeted for genocidal forays by Horthy's military, gendarmerie, and special units. Later, the same state organs persecuted Transylvanian Hungarians who stood up in defense of their Romanian and Jewish neighbors, and Hungarians with any kinship to Romanians. In three years at least 15,000 Transylvanian Romanians were murdered in the most brutal fashion, more than 280,000 Romanians were evicted from Transylvania, and about 150,000 Jews were deported to the Nazi death camp Auschwitz.

Many forced laborers lost their lives in so-called labor battalions. Numerous Romanian churches were devastated, the Romanian language was banned in schools, and Romanian names were Hungarianized.[81]

"I have seen almost the entire world, but the Romanian race is the only one that I disdain. In that country everyone is stealing, lying and using deception, and anyone can be bribed. In their short national history, they have betrayed all their allies and friends," wrote Horthy to Hitler in his April 1941 letter. In the same notice he pointed out that "once the immeasurable natural resources of Russia fall into German hands, we will be able to sustain to infinity."[82]

HORTHY'S UKRAINIAN GENOCIDE

Forcefully drafted Serbs and Slavs in general were excluded from Hungarian military units during forays to civilian populations in Ukraine and Belarus. Nazi criminals were certain that Slavic-origin soldiers would not become accomplices in browbeating their Slavic brethren.

In November 1943, the Hungarian Nazis in Ukraine went for "a chase on partisans." Prior to that foray, all Serbian soldiers were removed from the unit. After the "chase," Hungarians shamelessly boasted that they had encircled entire villages, killed everything that moved, and set the looted houses ablaze.[83]

When Pearl Harbor came under attack in December 1941, Horthy's Hungary declared war on the United States out of solidarity with Hitler. In the same month, England, having broken diplomatic relations with Hungary following the Hungarian invasion of Bachka, declared war on Hungary due to Horthy's refusal to quit his war campaign against the Soviet Union.[84]

Obsessed with fear of the Russians, Horthy was not capable of rational reasoning. In fact, the struggle against Russian Bolshevism was an excuse for everything he did during World War II.

VICTIMS OF HORTHY'S ANTI-SEMITISM

About 60,000 Hungarian Jews were murdered during their service in "labor battalions" on the Eastern Front and in an August 1941 massacre at Kamenets Podolsk.[85]

Following the Razzia in the winter of 1942, a member of the Exterior Committee, Gyergy Otlik, reported to Horthy in the fall of 1942 that he had been told during a visit to Germany that Hungary would do well if it did not wait on Germans to resolve the Jewish question, but to rather relocate the Jewish population eastward into occupied Russia. "Relocation" really implied execution, Otlik reported.[86]

In March 1944, Horthy agreed with Hitler to place 100,000 to 300,000 Hungarian Jews at disposal for "war production." The claim of some that Horthy had no idea about what was going on in Hungary fails before the very clear evidence we have. In 1948, a German Nazi leader named Veesenmayer stated the following during his trial:

Horthy himself told me that he was interested only in protecting those who were prosperous, the economically valuable Jews in Budapest, those who were well off. However, as to the remaining Jewry—and he used a very ugly term there—he had no interest in them and was quite prepared to have them go to the Reich or elsewhere for labor. He approved that; and he did not approve it after a demand made by me but he approved it after agreements and discussions with his premier and his ministers. The fact has been proved that he later—at first he moderated the deportations, and then later stopped them. Somebody who forbids something later on, must have given permission for it earlier.[87]

Hungarian criminal Laszlo Baku, one of Horthy's closest collaborators, ruthlessly carried out a speedy "final solution" in Hungary in 1944. While in prison, he wrote on April 7, 1945, that he issued a decree about ghettoizing the Jews following a request from Laszlo Endre, undersecretary of state directly responsible for deportations (as head of the administrative section of the ministry of interior). Endre submitted that request because "the regent [Horthy] agreed to turn the Jews over to the Germans for the sake of labor." Baku quotes Horthy's words to him:

Baku, you are one of my old Szeged officers. The Germans have cheated me. Now they want to deport the Jews. I don't mind. I hate the Galician Jews and the Communists. Out with them, out of the country! But you must see, Baku, that there are some Jews who are as good Hungarians as you and I. For example, here are little Chorin and Vida—aren't they good Hungarians? I can't allow these to be taken away. But they can take the rest![88]

Endre also testified, "The regent raised no objection to the deportations, saying that the sooner the operation was concluded, the sooner the Germans would leave the country."[89]

The ministry of exterior's telegram dated June 26, 1944, to Hungarian diplomatic representatives explained deportations of the Jews. The Hungarian government did not manage to compose a labor contingent for Germany, so now it was working "in accordance with the German request to place the Jews at their disposal." Thus, "based on the agreement, the Jews have been sent to Germany for the purpose of labor." The agreement was reached in Schloss Klessheim (in Upper Austria) on March 17, 1944. On the same occasion, Hitler informed Horthy about his decision to quietly occupy Hungary and prevent a betrayal similar to that of Italy. A Hungarian delegation was held against its will in Austria until the quiet occupation operation "Margareta" ended. In a conversation with Hitler, Horthy agreed to deport Hungarian Jews "for the purposes of labor."[90]

That Horthy was compliant with the extermination of the Jews was proved by a Protestant (Reformation) church priest, Laszlo Ravash. When he learned from the president of the Hungarian Upper House, Zhigmond Perenyi, about brutalities against the Jews during ghettoizing in Carpatho-Ruthenia (northeast Hungary), Ravash contacted Horthy to protest against such actions.

On April 28, 1944, Ravash met with Horthy who communicated to him that "a large number of labor draftees were requested from Hungary... A few hundred thousand Jews will leave the country's frontier in this manner, but not a single hair of their heads will be missing, just as is the case with the many hundreds of thousands of Hungarian workers who have been working in Germany since the beginning of the war." Horthy added that "laborers" would be dispatched along with their families so that they should not have to be "supported by our nation since the laborers are making a living out there."[91]

After the war, Ravash testified in Budapest about Miklos Horthy's actions, but the regent never faced justice for his policies of hatred toward the Jews, Serbs, Romanians, Russians, Ukrainians, Slavs in general, Roma, the poor, and the anti-Nazis.

Approximately 825,000 Jews (including 100,000 converts to Christianity, and Christians of Jewish origin considered to be Jews by the

Hungarian racist laws) lived in "Greater Hungary." Prior to Hitler's quiet occupation on March 19, 1944, Horthy had firm control over his state. To that very date, 42,000 Jewish slave laborers were murdered, as well as 20,000 "foreigners" (Jews without proof of Hungarian citizenship and Jewish refugees from Nazi-occupied European countries).[92] During the Razzia in Bachka, at least 241 Jews were murdered in Shaikashka villages, 189 in the town of Bechey, and 1,401 in the city of Novi Sad. Therefore, the number of victims of Horthy's anti-Semitic regime amounts to at least 63,831 individuals.

Following the Nazi German occupation of Hungary, with Horthy still as head of state prior to the "crossed arrows" (the Arrow Cross Party) that were later brought to power in October 1944, 618,007 Jews were deported to Nazi death camps.[93] German Nazis would never have been able to achieve the ethnic cleansing of Hungary without animated cooperation on the part of the Hungarian government, headed by Deme Stoyai, who was appointed prime minister with the consent of the head of state.

Miklos Horthy's rehabilitation advocates quote injustices of the Treaty of Versailles and hold to the fact that on July 7, 1944, the Hungarian regent suspended the deportation of the Jews.[94] At the same time, they forget that Horthy's politics and tolerance of anti-Semitism paved the way for all the deportations of the Jews to the German Nazi camps. Thus, in the period from May 15 to July 8, 1944, 440,000 Hungarian Jews were expedited to Auschwitz where they were murdered.[95]

German Nazi forces and Croatian Roman Catholic Ustasha units fought partisans at Frushka gora (a mountain in the province of Srem, on the other side of Danube facing Novi Sad, occupied by the Independent State of Croatia). The Hungarian Danube flotilla helped in the fight against those Serbian partisans which caused more victims of Horthy's Nazi regime.[96]

Historian Ishtwan Nemeshkirty, in his book *A Requiem for an Army*, wrote an indictment against Horthy and his generals regarding the downfall of the Hungarian army on the Eastern Front at the river Don. Out of 200,000, only 65,000 chilblained, crippled, and wounded soldiers returned after the greatest defeat that the Hungarian army had ever suf-fered. The defeat was even more horrendous considering that Hitler ordered that no soldier on the Eastern Front retreat in any way; all the troops on his side could march forward *only*.

The Second Hungarian Army that suffered that defeat was com-posed of forcefully drafted Serbs, Croats, Slovaks, poor Hungarian wage laborers, servants, and landless peasants. The Hungarians in that army were scorned. Both Horthy and the Hungarian aristocracy considered them a shame to the Hungarian nation.[97]

HORTHY'S GENOCIDAL RAID

The genocidal raid (or "Razzia") was a shocking crime against humanity. It had been carefully planned for months by Horthy and his accomplices and was executed in January of 1942. It began as a systematic murder of the civilian population in south Bachka settlements. It was an all-encompassing, brutal, premeditated massacre. The Razzia alone is sufficient to indict Miklos Horthy as a mass murderer of Serbs, Jews, Roma, and other innocent individuals.

The January 1942 Razzia, an alleged "combing of the terrain" to search for partisans, demonstrates the criminal profile of its patron through the fact that at least 310 children under age ten were slaughtered, as well as a great number of youth. Evidence of premeditated genocide was hurriedly and shamefully covered up after the war, and it is such an atrocious misdeed that an entire chapter must be devoted to it.

It is obvious that post-war Yugoslavia had put forth much effort to obliterate the memory of the genocidal January 1942 Razzia by diminishing the number of victims to senseless figures, dramatically reducing the proportions of the suffering of two ethnic groups: Serbs and Jews. A similar effort concealed the exact number and identity of victims of Hungarian and German descent who were massacred in Novi Sad, as well as the fact that the exact number of Roma victims has never been established. Post-war Yugoslav Communist history significantly diminished the proportions of the suffering of Ruthenians from the village of Gyurgyevo, while the number and identity of Slovaks summoned for incarceration on January 26, 1942, in the region of south Bachka is never mentioned.

A long-term struggle for the truth of the January 1942 genocide aims to preserve the memory of all the victims, regardless of their ethnic origin, as well as shed light on the chief commander—the perpetrator of a crime without precedence in Hungarian history—Miklos Horthy.

The decision to enact the so-called Razzia was made by the Hungarian regent himself following a suggestion from Ferentz Sombathely, commander of the Fifth National Corps in Szeged and the chief of staff, as documented in the Regional Commission for Establishing the Crimes Committed by the Occupiers and their Domestic Collaborators in Vojvodina (Chapter III, mass murders, Razzia [murders and massacres: systematic terror, torture of civilians, rape and plunder])—MSRB No. 2115 compiled in October 11, 1945, the Archive No. R 1938 (Introduction).[1] It is difficult to convey the extent of the suffering inflicted upon the people of southern Bachka by the enactment of Horthy's decision.

According to data obtained by Endre Baichy Zhilinsky, in the Shaikashka region (a geographic triangle in southern Bachka formed by the rivers Tisa and Danube), in the city of Novi Sad, and the towns of Srobran and Bechei, a total of at least 12,763 citizens died by Horthy's command in January 1942.

JANUARY 1942: RAZZIA IN SHAIKASHKA

Superhuman efforts I have put forth in collecting and processing the data on Razzia victims have so far resulted in 1,499 identified victims from Shaikashka villages.[2] Unfortunately, the identity of many victims, primarily those from Churug and Zhabaly colonies, cannot be established because the representatives of Horthy's state annihilated entire families and stocks.

The building in Gyurgyevo from whence the victims of the Razzia of that village were taken to the riverbank of the Tisa, murdered, and thrown under the ice of the frozen river. The building was located on the grounds of the elementary school. It was demolished in 2010 by order of the school principal.

In Vilovo colony, the smallest one in Shaikashka region, the occupiers prescribed 80 villagers for liquidation. There were sixty-five individuals murdered by the Hungarian Nazis. Eight of those were minors (one a child under ten). In January 1942, the Hungarian Nazis killed many agricultural peasants and housekeepers (a large number of people from those classes were murdered in all Shaikashka villages), as well as a clerk, two tradesmen, a notary, a judge, a village order monitor, a butcher, a cafe bar owner, and an innkeeper.

The village of Gardinovtzy is located at the Danube riverside, thus the fate of 47 identified victims from that village is quite clear. Among Gardinovtzy victims were two minors. In the assault on the civilian population, Horthy's hordes exterminated agriculturalists and housekeepers, a village midwife, a notary, a fisherman, a monk, an innkeeper, a teacher, three merchants, and four tradesmen.

Based on available data, Horthy's regular soldiers and gendarmes executed 95 citizens of the village of Gospodyintzy. Because the local

Orthodox Church composed a list of victims, it can be adequately assumed that probably all individuals murdered in the Razzia 1942 in that village have been identified to the last victim, considering the pedantic approach the church usually takes regarding such matters. There were twenty minors among the victims (including a couple of victims under ten). The "valiant" Horthy soldiers fighting "the partisans" left Gospody-intzy in January 1942 without two clerks, a notary, a priest, a physician, six merchants, three artisans, a worker, a lawyer, a police commander, agriculturalists, and housekeepers.

Based on the oldest Serbian document on "cleansing of the ground" and testimonies given by witnesses and relatives of the victims of the genocide sponsored by Miklos Horthy, the identities of 344 victims from the village of Gyurgyevo have been established. This crucial fact

Vladimir Erdelyi, a Ruthenian from the village of Gyurgyevo. He was captured by the Hungarian military, brutally tortured, and later hung. This photo was taken in December 1940.

The wedding portrait of Milan and Rose Yovanov. He was a pharmacist in Zhabaly. Both were murdered in the Razzia that occurred there.

confirms the veracity of the claim made in the document that about 350 victims had been murdered in that village. Due to the outstanding success achieved by my Holocaust and genocide research, as I followed the trail of the earliest Serbian document about the Razzia 1942, it can be unequivocally claimed that the largest number of Gyurgyevo victims have been identified. Among these were three clerks, an agronomist, three notaries, nine teachers, a priest, fifteen merchants, twenty-seven craftsmen, two pharmacists, a physician, a writer, a shepherd, a female student, a young poet, Leona Erdelyi, and numerous housekeepers, agriculturalists, pupils, and children. Ten young Gyurgyevo men were murdered in direct skirmishes with their genocidal occupiers. The scale of the Nazi forces' foray on Gyurgyevo and the monstrosity of Horthy's ideology that led them, is obvious from the fact that among the murdered villagers were 80 minors (including twenty-five children under ten).

My special thanks always goes to late Michael Hornyak, a native of Gyurgyevo, a diplomat of former Yugoslavia to the Far East. He has pro-vided me invaluable information about local conditions and population, as well as memories of his relatives, neighbors, and classmates murdered by the Hungarian occupiers.

In Zhabaly village, the Hungarian state apparatus attacked, with an acrid brutality, the unarmed civilian popula-tion, immediately after having neutral-ized an insignificant "Shaikashka partisan squad" that was encamped at Zhabaly municipality. So far, I have identified only 795 victims out of 3,500 mur-dered villagers. The number of 3,500 is the claim in one of the earliest writings about the Razzia.[3] The victims included 151 minors (49 of whom were children

Georg Zhivanov, a priest in Zhabaly. He was taken by the Hungarian occupiers and murdered on the bank of the Tisa River on January 5, 1942. His body was dumped into the river.

A church fresco featuring the victims of the Razzia in the village of Lok.

under ten). Other than agriculturalists and housekeepers, who make up the greatest number of murdered victims in the Shaikashka region, Hungarian forces also murdered sixty-eight craftsmen, forty-three merchants, thirteen workers, ten clerks, five lawyers, three Orthodox priests, four physicians, five students, twelve innkeepers, a widow, three shepherds, four teachers, a pressman, a military captain, a road keeper, a custody guardian, four notaries, a miller, two cadets, a parish clerk, a church singer, a pharmacist, a photographer, a road inspector, a veterinarian, an embankment keeper, an embankment guardian, a chauffeur, and a couple of servants. The Nazis killed only twelve active resistance movement members in their annihilation foray.

Of the victims from the Shaikashka village of Lok, fifty-two have been identified. During the so-called Razzia, the Hungarian Nazis murdered a merchant, nine craftsmen, an embankment guardian, a notary, a teacher, a forester, a factory inspector, two innkeepers, an officer, a road keeper, and a policeman.

Based on available documents, it has been recently established that Horthy's forces in Moshorin massacred 236 victims. Numerous documents have been preserved as a testimony to the attentive preparation for "combing the area" that these forces used, far in advance of the January pogrom. Insight into the entire tragedy and genocidal plan of the January Razzia 1942 may be understood when one considers the number of young people under eighteen, the elderly, and the peaceful, ordinary citizens who were slain. Many criminals that participated in the genocidal January Razzia escaped justice. Horthy's men in Moshorin massacred fifty-one individuals under eighteen (among

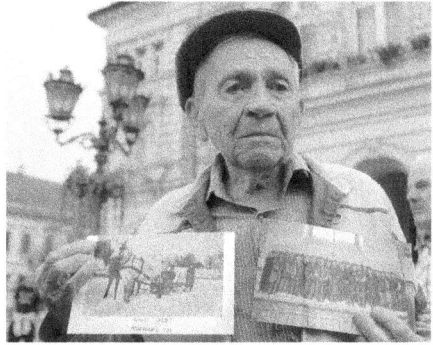

Lyubisha Letich, a survivor of the Lok pogrom. He is shown holding a photograph of the horses the Nazi occupiers used to take his father away from home. His father was murdered in the Razzia

those were twenty-eight children under ten). In addition to house-keepers and agriculturalists, the Hungarian state apparatus, in its bloody

Lyubitza Maletin, a teacher in the village of Moshorin, and her children. All were murdered in the Razzia in Moshorin by Horthy's Nazi troops. Before the teacher was killed, her daughter was raped and murdered before her eyes.

foray, annihilated three students, two grave diggers, seven craftsmen, five merchants, two workers, a policeman, a clergyman, an Orthodox priest, a priest's maid who was ethnic Hungarian, a professor, a lower notary, a teacher, a water-way guardian, and a landowner.

In Temerin, Hungarian forces called on all the local Jews to report to the municipal center. Those who were not at home were sent a telegram instructing them to report as soon as they returned. A family of mixed Serbian and Hungarian origin was collected with the Jews. They were transported by night to the bank of the Tisa in the district of Zhabaly. That savage crime claimed 50 identified victims. In addition to housekeepers and agriculturalists, the Nazis "cleansed" Temerin in January 1942 of a pharmacist, seven merchants, a chemistry engineer, two clerks and two physicians. Among them were seven minors under ten. The cold-blooded slaying of the young marks this crime with exceptional brutality.

The Nazi January Razzia 1942 in Titel was carried out quietly. It is worth noting that women and children were not murdered in that pogrom, even though one minor was killed. The Nazis murdered fifty-nine identified victims: a parish clerk, an Orthodox priest, an innkeeper, a student, a river canal guardian, an officer, a physician, a teacher, two merchants, a worker, four artisans, a bookshop owner, two servants, three clerks, and several agriculturalists. Andrash Lukach, an ethnic Hungarian, leader of the local anti-Horthy resistance movement, was also arrested, taken to Novi Sad, and later shot. It is possible to have a good insight into the nature of the Horthy regime's policy of extermination: The executors of the Churug Razzia 1942, in the bitter cold of January, uprooted 142 youth under eighteen (including 20 children under ten). Of all Churug villagers, thirty-five percent were annihilated in the Razzia 1942, while less than half of the victims have been identified (1,360 out of 3,800). Among the victims were eighty-six artisans, sixty-eight merchants, twenty-five workers, two lawyers, three students, two millers, two clerks, a rabbi, a chauffeur, four physicians, a servant, a school janitor, two chimney sweeps, two Orthodox priests, thirteen innkeepers, six clerks, two pharmacists, a technician, a notary, four teachers, two cattlemen, three landowners, an agronomy engineer, a district treasurer, a clergyman, a cab driver, a beer factory owner, a lower notary, a canton commissioner, two railway workers, a soda maker, a fisherman, a river canal custodian, numerous agriculturalists and housekeepers, as well as fourteen members of resistance movements.

A photo of the Gestapo file kept on Magdalene Weiss, nee Lampel, who lived in the territory occupied by the German Nazis. After being deported from the town of Panchevo to Belgrade, she managed to escape with her two sons and reach Churug (under Hungarian occupation) where her parents lived. The Hungarian occupiers murdered the entire families of Lampel and Weiss in the Churug Razzia.

Sigmund Handler, who rushed to Budapest to warn authorities that the Razzia in Churug had begun, hoping that his intervention would halt the genocide in that largest of Shaikashka villages. He was murdered for his efforts in a Budapest prison. Handler is pictured above, seated in front, second from left, wearing a bow tie.

Following the Orthodox Christmas liturgy in the village of Shaikash, a Hungarian officer intercepted local attendees and read out names from a list composed by local members of Kulturbund (the German Nazi movement in Vojvodina). Local ethnic Germans led the Hungarian Nazis to arrest Margita Shlesinger and other locals who did not attend the church mass. Twenty-seven of the victims have been identified. In addition to agriculturalists and housekeepers, who comprised the majority of victims in the village, a police officer and a student (a member of the resistance movement) were also murdered.

JANUARY RAZZIA 1942 IN NOVI SAD

In the Novi Sad raid, Horthy's hordes executed over 5,000 individuals. Less than half of the victims—2,370 only—have been identified by name and/or certain biographical data, despite the painstaking work of my research and fact finding. Among the victims are 338 identified youth under eighteen. Along with numerous housekeepers, 29 students, 76 clerks, 120 merchants, 17 lawyers, 12 physicians, and 22 teachers were murdered.

The Novi Sad Razzia, a genocide carried out on January 21-23, 1942, was absolutely planned in advance and approved by Miklos Horthy, just as in the previous, government-controlled occupation in the Shaikashka villages around Novi Sad. The Hungarian state's highest organs were in total control of the situation in the field, which is obvious from the fact that a Novi Sad Jew, Zhigmund Handler, was murdered in Budapest where he had traveled promptly, in the hope of persuading authorities to stop the Razzia in Churug that had begun on January 4, 1942. The fact that Dr. Handler was then murdered in a Budapest prison shows that both Horthy and his government were willing initiators of the so-called Razzia in South Bachka.

Dr. Handler ran to Budapest immediately once the massacre of civilians had begun in Churug village. The purpose of his trip was to explain that a mistake was in process that was causing the unwarranted suffering of ordinary citizens. Like many others, Dr. Handler could not believe that a senseless massacre was unfolding in Horthy's well-organized state. Budapest authorities executed Dr. Handler in the Hungarian capital, while his family was annihilated in Novi Sad on January 23, 1942.[4] The Holocaust Memorial Society concludes that the way Dr. Handler was treated by the Budapest Hungarian local authorities is one of the most crucial proofs that all levels of Hungarian authorities—including the head of state, Horthy—were well aware of what was going on in the field. On the third day of the killing spree, January 23, 1942, the largest number of Novi Sad victims of "terrain combing" were permanently uprooted. The Novi Sad river beach (the Strand) has remained an unmarked murder site, still used for summer and winter amusement activities, even though it was one of the most gruesome killing grounds of World War II.

It is significant to note that in the Novi Sad Razzia, 214 Jewish youth and 110 youth of other ethnic origins have been identified as victims. The enormous number of Jewish youth killed proves that there was a particular hunting of Novi Sad Jews, and that Horthy made an effort to emulate the German Nazi leader and Hitler's satellites (the Roman Catholic Independent State of Croatia and Slovakia) and uproot as many Jews as possible. Since there are cherished theories that the highest offices in Hungary were not aware of the Razzia 1942, nor did they have any influence on its course in the field, the first paragraph of an announcement posted in Novi Sad right after the Razzia is important to keep in mind. That announcement was signed by the Hungarian military commander, who wrote that on January 23, 1942, a delegation of the Novi Sad mayor and civic representatives visited him in the evening and pleaded that "at the end of investigation of the Communist partisans and other enemies of the Hungarian state, ordered by the Hungarian Royal Government, the army should restore order in the city as soon as possible." The Hungarian regent always attended all sessions of the Hungarian government. (Section II of this book provides much greater detail concerning the Novi Sad January Razzia.)

RAZZIA 1942 IN SRBOBRAN

The citizens of Srbobran who survived the April 1941 persecution and pogrom experienced a new wave of terror on January 25, 1942, when three individuals succumbed to torture. They were Paya Tamburashev, Karlo Flaishmann, a teacher, and Isidor Shiyachich, a butcher.

RAZZIA 1942 IN KISACH

Horthy's forces carried out an action described as a "raid" on January 26, 1942, in order to arrest members of the resistance from Kisach, a village populated by ethnic Slovaks. The persecutors took away 150 villagers, among whom were the wives of resistance movement members who had successfully evaded all Nazi searches throughout the war. According to Pavel Bartok's testimony, the majority of imprisoned villagers—ethnic Slovaks—never returned after the "raid."

RAZZIA 1942 IN BECHEY

The last link in the chain of horrible genocidal actions was a systematic massacre of Bechey citizens. The lure of booty and the theory that there were three adequate places for Serbs—"gallows, Danube and Tisa"—constantly preoccupied the local Hungarian Nazis in spite of the fact that numerous local ethnic Hungarians (who formed the majority population in the town) resisted the pogrom. Many neighbors did not heed the warnings from their Hungarian fellow citizens to leave the town.

They could not believe that any kind of massacre was possible in a town that had always had harmonious ethnic relations. Many ethnic Hungarians in Bechey were part of the anti-Nazi movement prior to World War II. Since the occupiers did not manage to cause divisions among the citizens, they arrived at the conclusion they should annihilate and plunder as many as they wished.

Even though all the citizens after the war were aware of the fact that more than 300 individuals were thrown into the Tisa, the efforts to falsify history had also embroiled Bechey, with an aim to reduce that number below 300.[5] So far, 380 victims have been identified. At the end of January 1942, Bechey lost twenty-four youth under eighteen. The Hungarian occupiers threw the following under the ice: a municipal vice notary, a military officer, a construction contractor, forty-four merchants, thirteen clerks, three workers, fifteen artisans, five physicians, two students, two high school students, one innkeeper, three economists, a bookkeeper, two butchers, a shipping agent, four lawyers, a French professor, a steersman, a police officer, a beggar, a synagogue janitor, a machinist, a road keeper, an engineer, a law student, a Jewish cantor, housekeepers, and farmers. Of all these victims, only four were active members of the resistance movement against Horthy's Nazism.

During a session of the Hungarian Parliament, a minister in Horthy's government, Miklosh Kalai, "admitted" that 2,550 Serbs altogether were killed in the Razzia of 1942.[6]

Following the Razzia in Novi Sad, Horthy's authorities formed a commission for registration of the property of "missing individuals." The goal of the Hungarian

Lyubitza Loncharsky, a young lady from Churug, murdered in the Churug Razzia. Her body was thrown into the Tisa River and later found by a fisherman from another village, who retrieved this photo from a pocket of her coat. After the war, the fisherman brought the photo to Churug to ask if anyone knew who she was.

state was to seize the property of the victims. According to a statement made by the Hungarian government in January 27, 1942, 6,000 to 7,000 Serbs were slain.[7]

Certain individuals find it difficult to accept that the regent of Hungary was well aware of the Razzia. They would rather believe that the genocide was committed by Hungarian military troops without Horthy's knowledge and approval. However, even the staunchest unbelievers will remain without any argument when faced with the proof discovered by English historian Carlile Macartney. His written document unambiguously points out the person behind the massacre of innocent civilians in the Bachka region.

In expectation of a forthcoming judicial process against Novi Sad Razzia 1942 perpetrators, Horthy's chief of martial office, general Layosh Kerestesh-Fischer, brother of the then minister of interior, wrote an encouraging note to one of the main culprits, Ferentz Feketehalmy Tzaydner. In that letter, which Macartney discovered after World War II, Horthy's chief of martial office wrote the following, "Even if an investigation against you should be initiated, Horthy will stand in your support."[8]

The message to Tzaydner precisely depicts the monstrous duplicity of Miklos Horthy. "Even if an investigation should be initiated" underscores the fact that Horthy was doing everything within his power to thwart an investigation. Therefore, it is no wonder that he later ordered that the investigation be suspended! "Horthy will stand in your support"—that is, he would stand in support of the murderers, plunderers, rapists, anti-Semites, Serb-haters, and Slavic-haters that had been led by Tzaydner.

Horthy's martial office chief unwittingly denounced the regent of Hungary through this message. While Horthy had been pretending not to know—putting on a wholesome face, in the face of genocide and hatred for anything and everything non-Hungarian—he in fact supported odium for those "unreliable elements" for whom he had not even the slightest feeling of empathy or mercy.

In the battle for Stalingrad, the Soviet army launched a full-scale offensive against Nazi troops. The offensive affected the Hungarian troops stationed at the river Don around the city of Voronyezh. In the combat that transpired from January 12 to January 30, 1943, the Second Hungarian Army lost 147,871 soldiers.[9] That was one of many tragic consequences of Horthy's political alliance with Hitler.

HORTHY PAVED THE WAY TO THE CROSSED ARROWS

Because of his tendencies to approach the Western Allies, Horthy became of no use to Hitler and was politically neutralized on March 19, 1944. On March 22, Hitler appointed an altogether Nazi Hungarian government, and an immediate ban on all civic parties that had been opposed to Horthy ensued. Jews were ordered to wear yellow armbands, concentration ghettoes opened in April 1944, and a mass deportation of Jews to Nazi death camps commenced in the summer.[1]

In July 1944, the First Hungarian Army was defeated at Lyvov, Ukraine. Following the capitulations of Finland, Bulgaria, and Romania in August and September of 1944, Nazi Hungary and the Roman Catholic Independent State of Croatia remained Hitler's sole European allies. On October 15, 1944, Horthy appealed over the radio to the Hungarian army to establish a truce and cooperate with Soviet troops at the front. The military headquarters did not forward those instructions to the troops, because, by that time, the Hungarian army had been completely overrun by a pro-Nazi cadre.[2] The night of Horthy's radio appeal, German parachutists stormed the royal palace and forced the Hungarian regent to convey his regency mandate to a Hitlerite, Ferentz Salashi.

In service to the Reich, Salashi declared a conscription of age fourteen to sixty, while the gold reserves of the Hungarian National Bank were transferred to Germany. He was even preparing a total evacuation of the Hungarian population to Germany. During his totalitarian reign, Nazi mobs murdered 10,000 political opponents, and about 80,000 Budapest Jews were deported to German Nazi death camps. Horthy's power paved the way for the worst Nazi leader (up to that point) in the history of the Hungarian people.[3]

OBSESSION WITH BORDER REVISION

A former top informant in Horthy's headquarters, Gyula Kadar, pointed out an important trait of Horthy's in his memoirs. He writes:

> As a close observer, I have to give a wider retrospective of our inglorious past and preposterous political agenda and to explain why such a political agenda was doomed to failure. With numerous examples I intend to depict the ever deepening slime and overall powerlessness that Horthy's politics were sinking into, as well as to underline nonplus [or baffling] position of a system whose sole aim was to revise the borders.

A Serbian author who analyzed Kadar's writings and spoke with him face to face concludes:

> The most relevant characteristic of Horthy and his men in power was that their sentiments ranged from moderate to extremely aggressive. The common trait of all was that in moments when they thought they might gain something if they were coupled with the politics of one mightier than they (at first with Mussolini's Italy, later with Hitler, or rather with both dictators at one point), the appetites of that irredentist clique rose to indescribable proportions. In those moments, they would lose connection with reality and rush into a catastrophe caused by the inadequately designed vision of a Hungary they desired and aimed for. And when reality had demolished all their hopes and buried all their dreams, then—even at times of the deepest despair—they did not pull all their strength to at least redirect heading of the entire nation to its tragedy.[4]

REVIVAL OF HORTHY'S IDEOLOGY

An article authored by Predrag Lastich, Vice President of the Serbian Autonomous Community in Budapest, is cause for concern regarding the attitude of the Hungarian people toward Serbia and Serbs. Among other things, the Serbian nation is demonized in Hungarian history textbooks; whereas other minority communities "are rarely mentioned, often in negative context," Serbs "are the only ethnic group that is mentioned only in negative context."[1] A survey of Hungarian students in the year 2000 showed they harbored great disdain toward Serbs.

After World War II, the Orthodox temples in Hungary were expropriated from the Serbian Orthodox Church in the period from 1948 to 1953. Serbian religious schools in Hungary were seized by the state. The autonomy of Serbian civic schools was abolished. The Serbian cultural institutions and legacies were turned into state property. Two thirds of the Serbian pieces of art and valuable sacral objects had vanished. At the end of World War I, there remained only forty of seventy Serbian Orthodox churches. Some of those church buildings were sold to other religious communities when ethnic Serbs moved to the newly formed Yugoslav state in 1918. The Serbian national corpus mostly dissipated into the Baranya region, thus several Orthodox churches were razed.

After World War I, two thirds to three quarters of 25,000 to 30,000 Serbs opted to move from Hungary to former Yugoslavia.[2]

In 2005, obligatory use of the Hungarian language was introduced into the workplaces of minority communities. Thus, a legalized assimilation of the remaining Serbian population came into force. Officially, the fate of thirty-seven cultural cenotaphs (tombs, cemeteries, monuments, prisons, and camps from the two world wars) is unknown.[3]

HORTHY'S CONTEMPORARY SUPPORTERS

On June 7, 2009, the Serbian daily *Evening News* (*Vecernje Novosti*) published an article entitled "Perilous Games with Border Lines in Europe." At that time the former Hungarian Prime Minister Victor Orban appealed to Hungarian national communities in the surrounding countries to vote as many Hungarian deputies as possible into the European Parliament, so that those delegates could strive for "the Hungarian cause that is inseparable from autonomy." The leader of then Hungarian opposition Fides party exhorted his kinsmen to strive for the interests of the Carpathian Basin (that is, Greater Hungary) which, in turn, caused distrust from the neighbors. The following sentence in the article shows that such was not the first incident of that nature: "Budapest's sorrow over the lands it lost in World War I has again disturbed its neighbors."[4]

LIABILITY AND BLOOD GUILTINESS

In Report No. 89, the National Commission (for establishing crimes committed by the occupiers and their domestic collaborators) cites the crime of forceful drafting of Bachka citizens into the Hungarian army. The first culprit listed is "Miklos Horthy, the Regent of Hungary and Hungarian Chief of Staff ." The report cites names of the minister of the military, the head of the military headquarters, the headquarters supervisor, and others. The National Commission made that record on Miklos Horthy's crimes on January 13, 1946.

The National Commission, in Report No. 90, concluded that several individuals were culpable of "the systematic destruction of our population by the means of brutal slave labor that was imposed by Hungarian occupiers." The first culpable person listed for that crime is "Horthy, Miklos, Regent of Hungary and Hungarian Chief of Staff."[5] In the closing comments of that record, which was also penned on January 13, 1946, the National Commission emphasized that regarding the listed perpetrators, "the commission believes that all of those must be brought to the courts…in order to experience just punishment."

The Regional Commission for establishing the crimes of occupiers and their domestic collaborators wrote, in the introduction of its 1946 report, that

> *Horthy and his collaborators had perfidiously and traitorously attacked our territory pretending that they had to 'open the gates of the dungeon where 300,000 of their brethren were imprisoned', while, in fact, they shielded the chauvinistic, megalomaniacal and Fascist scum; thus, united 'liberators' turned Baranya and Bachka into a real dungeon and a huge sepulcher where they buried tens of thousands of Vojvodina people.*

The Regional Commission notes 50,000 overall victims who fell at various murder sites and more than 280,000 forcefully detained, drafted, arrested, and abused victims of Horthy's terror. In the first chapter of the Regional Commission's report, it is said that Horthy and his collaborators were "mass murderers" and the crimes committed by them were "planned and premeditated" against "the population of Slavic and Jewish origin" who were unarmed and innocent victims. At the end of an exhaustive report, the commission wrote a chapter entitled, "The list of so far established notable war criminals in army, gendarmerie and police forces." The very first liable person listed is "Horthy, Miklos, the Regent of Hungary."

As far as responsibility for the death of victims during the April 1941 invasion of Bachka, the Regional Commission concluded that "the following individuals must be tried and convicted as war criminals: Horthy, Miklos, Regent of Hungary, as the Supreme Commander of the Hungarian Army" as well as other military personnel.

GUILTY AS ANY NAZI LEADER

The committee of chief prosecutors of the International Military Tribunal in Nuremberg was the first body to use and define the term "genocide" in the judicial process against Nazi criminals. From any point of view, their definition perfectly fits the doings of Miklos Horthy. Chief prosecutors at Nuremberg determined that indicted Nazi leaders "carried out an intentional and systematic genocide, that is, the annihilation of racial and national groups, civilian population in certain occupied areas, aiming to destroy certain races and classes of population, as well as national, racial or religious groups, particularly Jews, Poles, Gypsies and others" [in Horthy's case, Serbs as well].[6]

What is the essence of genocide—its legal nature? Genocide as a legal term was coined within the international law community when the UN Convention was adopted. National legislations drew their respective regulations from that convention. The essence of genocide is comprised of a couple of elements: murder, destruction, or annihilation; and the national, racial, or religious origin or qualification of those destroyed. Without cumulative existence of those two characteristics, an act cannot be considered genocide, but is treated as a crime of another nature. The essence of genocide is that the annihilator undertakes a series of measures and actions connected into a system, with a clear aim to uproot physically or biologically, totally or partly, a national, religious, or ethnic group. Therefore, genocide is characterized by a systematic approach to destroying ethnic or religious groups as opposed to sporadic war crimes. In the actions of Miklos Horthy, both traits of the crime of genocide have been demonstrated.

HORTHY EVADED MOSCOW DECLARATION

The great powers (the United States, the United Kingdom, and the Soviet Union) signed the Moscow Declaration on October 30, 1943, with the resolution that, after the war, Nazi war criminals were to be sent back to countries in which they committed war crimes in order to be tried and punished according to the laws of those countries. In the cases of those major criminals whose offenses had no particular geographical location, it was decided by the Declaration that they would be punished by a joint decision of the governments of the Allies.

Justice provided by the Moscow Declaration did not encompass Miklos Horthy and numerous Hungarians criminals.

Even more interesting was the fact that the International Military Court at Nuremberg tried crimes like those committed by Horthy but did not prosecute the genocidal Hungarian regent. The Court's Principles represent the first document that combined crimes against humanity with crimes forbidden by international law. Principle VI states that the International Military Court would prosecute the following:

a. Crimes against peace:
    i.   Planning, preparation, initiation or waging of a war of aggression or a war in violation of international treaties, agreements or assurances;
    ii. Participation in a common plan or conspiracy for the accomplishment of any of the acts mentioned under (i).

b. War crimes:

    Violations of the laws or customs of war which include, but are not limited to, murder, ill-treatment or deportation of slave labor or for any other purpose of the civilian population of or in occupied territory; murder or ill-treatment of prisoners of war or persons on the Seas, killing of hostages, plunder of public or private property...

c. Crimes against humanity:

    Murder, extermination, enslavement, deportation, and other inhuman acts done against any civilian population, or persecutions on political, racial, or religious grounds, when such acts are done or such persecutions are carried on in execution of or in connection with any crime against peace or any war crime."

The Hungarian Penal Code from 1978 (Article 156, paragraph II) provides that a person who prepares a genocide "is doing a criminal deed and will be punished by a duress to last from two to eight years." The Portuguese Penal Code from 1983, in the section dealing with crimes against peace and humanity (Article 189), provides that a crime of genocide and racial discrimination implies "murder of the members of a society or a group" and "severe assault on physical or psychological integrity of the members of a society or a group." A person who commits such a crime is to be imprisoned for a term "ranging from ten to twenty-five years."[7]

LIABILITY ACCORDING TO INTERNATIONAL LAW

Article 4 of the UN Convention on the Prevention and Punishment of the Crime of Genocide clearly specifies that all genocide and other crime perpetrators covered by the Convention will be liable "whether they are constitutionally responsible rulers, public officials or private individuals." Although the Convention was adopted in 1948 (while Horthy was alive), Hungary's responsible ruler and statesman was not brought into account for his numerous systematic genocidal crimes. This is even more indicative of an even greater injustice toward the victims if viewed in light of Article 7 of the Constitution of the International Military Court that greatly influenced the final formulation of the UN Convention. The aforementioned Article 7 of the Constitution of the International Military Court states the following, "The official position of defendants, whether as Heads of State or responsible officials in Government Departments, shall not be considered as freeing them from responsibility or mitigating punishment."

By Legal Decree No. 27, Hungary declared in 1964 that prosecution of war criminals and execution of punishment for such crimes cannot be superannuated if a perpetrator is sentenced to fifteen or more years in prison.[8]

Miklos Horthy died in Portugal on February 9, 1957. He willed his remains not to be returned to his birthplace as long as "the last Russian soldier" remained on Hungarian soil. Two years after the retreat of the last Russian soldiers, Horthy's descendants fulfilled his behest in 1993.

HORTHY'S CRIMES UNDER NON-APPLICABILITY OF STATUTORY LIMITATIONS

The United Nations Convention on the Non-Applicability of Statutory Limitations to War Crimes and Crimes Against Humanity stipulates no statutory limitation shall apply to such crimes, irrespective of the date of their commission! The Convention enumerates the crimes under the Constitution of the International Military Tribunal at Nuremberg. Article 2 of the Convention states,

> ...the provisions of this Convention shall apply to representatives of the State authority and private individuals who, as principals or accomplices, participate in or who directly incite others to the commission of any of those crimes, or who conspire to commit them, irrespective of the degree of completion, and to representatives of the State authority who tolerate their commission.

According to enforced international law, as stated in the UN Convention on the Non-Applicability of Statutory Limitations to War Crimes and Crimes Against Humanity (adopted and opened for signature, ratification, and accession by General Assembly resolution 2391 (XXIII) of 26 November 1968, entered into force on 11 November 1970), Miklos Horthy is guilty of inciting genocide over non-Hungarian nations. Having been a Hungarian state authority, he is also guilty of tolerating commission of genocide and later helping to free the culprits. The crimes of Miklos Horthy are subject to non-applicability of statutory limitations and have not been superannuated.

INDICTMENT BY ENDRE BAICHY ZHILINSKY

When he learned of the Shaikashka massacre that was carried out from January 4-19, 1942, a Hungarian deputy, Endre Baichy Zhilinsky, addressed the Hungarian Prime Minister Laszlo Bardoshy because he learned from reliable sources that Horthy's military was going to commit crimes in the city of Novi Sad as well. Zhilinsky appealed to Bardoshy on January 21, 1942, which means there was sufficient time to prevent new crimes had the highest Hungarian authorities the will to do so. Instead, the slaughter of civilians in Novi Sad (January 21-23, 1942) and Bechey (January 27-29, 1942) ensued.

It is a commonly held belief that deputy Zhilinsky addressed the Hungarian regent believing he was not versed with events in the field, but there is no obvious evidence in support of that. Zhilinsky's sources came from Hungarian military circles, and his personal Serbian friends in Bachka, so he would not presume that a person in Horthy's position was not well versed in what was going on in or outside of the state.

In his memorandum to Horthy dated February 4, 1942, Zhilinsky described the pogrom in the Shaikashka region and brought his attention to the fact that later in Novi Sad "the entire pogrom was basely planned, prepared in advance and there is enormous evidence to support that claim."

"In some streets they have annihilated the entire Serbian and Jewish families" notes Zhilinsky, and claims that someone has to be held accountable.

During the Hungarian parliament sessions, risking his personal safety, Zhilinsky persistently asked for accountability. His memorandum represents the best indictment against the regent of Hungary:

> As far as I am aware, in these one thousand years there has been no official pogrom in Hungary, incited by or in collaboration with the state organs of power… A sheer official pogrom without any indictment and with the exclusion of defense, as well as mass murders in a grandiose style may be recorded in Hungarian history in January 1942, to the

eternal shame of Hungariandom, of the nation, of Hungarian legal state, of Hungarian spirit, of humanity and of Christian inspiration of Saint Stephen's Europeandom…

In a subtitle of his memorandum, "Political Accountability and Liability," Zhilinsky wrote the following:

Someone has to be held accountable for these unspeakable abominations and odium; someone has to be liable for Shaikashka and Novi Sad pogroms committed by the incentive, approval and collaboration of the military. In fact, many must be held accountable, some politically and others for committed crimes. Political responsibility rests on the heads of the prime minister and the government, namely the minister of military, the minister of interior and the minister of justice. From political accountability stems their duty to place no impediments and to open the way without any scrupula for the realization of liability, primarily for the sake of settling the issues of who was the top principal factor that instigated and nurtured this pogrom…First the main culprit has to be destroyed and only then those mini sadists.

"The main culprit" was not destroyed, nor was there a mention of him in school classes, Serbian and Jewish historical records, or protocols of commemorative speeches. In vain was the cry for justice from the honest man Zhilinsky. His memorandum to Horthy is a timeless testimony. Nations that Miklos Horthy tried to exterminate have a moral obligation to pluck from oblivion this forgotten criminal and his many crimes.

"It is my deepest conviction that the last moment for action has come!" ends Zhilinsky's impassioned plea to Horthy.[9]

The moment to snatch from historical oblivion one of the worst criminal offenders of the Second World War is speedily running out. Rehabilitation of Miklos Horthy's legacy will inevitably entail revival and rationalization of his crimes. This would be a terrible thing for humanity, because those who forget their history are condemned to repeat it.

SECTION II

The Great Raid on Novi Sad

INTRODUCTION TO SECTION II

The truth is sometimes painful and frightening. Good inter-ethnic relations and peace are able to grow only in truth. In this case, a brutal genocide was committed during the Second World War by the Hungarian occupation forces in the northern Serbian city of Novi Sad, the administrative center of the region of Bachka. For eight long decades, that event has been hidden in European history. It was named the "Razzia" (or *Great Raid*).

Hungarian Nazis hung a Hungarian deputy, Endre Baichy Zhilinsky, because he persistently demanded justice in the Hungarian Parliament for the victims who were murdered in Novi Sad by Horthy's forces on January 21-23, 1942. In that genocide, over 5,000 Novi Sad residents were brutally murdered and tossed under the ice into the Danube River; their only "crime" was that they were not ethnically Hungarians, but Serbs, Jews, Roma, or of Slavic origin. Anti-Nazi Germans and Hungarians were also murdered.

Several years ago, I had an encounter with the truth about the Novi Sad Razzia. The more I analyzed the depth of a war crime that had no precedent in Serbian history, the more I discerned the scope of this horrific genocide. I was shocked by the realization that the official figures were deliberately falsified.

The stories of the victims and their sufferings were the drive that led me to investigate the official half-truths. In that process, I also discovered Zhilinsky, a European visionary of that time. I discovered many great people like him as well. Among those are Layosh Dunafalvi and Andor Molnar (who rescued the village of Kovily from genocide), Germans who rescued the village of Kach, the Hungarians who rescued the villages of Nadaly and Budisava, as well as a myriad of "little" people of Novi Sad—janitors, cooks, and servants—who rescued their neighbors. I admire their example during those perilous times.

RELIABLE INTERNATIONAL DOCUMENTS ABOUT THE NUMBER OF JANUARY RAZZIA 1942 VICTIMS

1

CHAPTER

A VISIONARY FOR OUR TIME

Due to the efforts of Hungarian deputy Endre Baichy Zhilinsky, it was established that the Hungarian Nazi raids in 1942 in the Shaikashka region surrounding Novi Sad and the city of Novi Sad itself claimed at least 12,763 victims.[1] Following are excerpts from Zhilinsky's memorandum to the Hungarian regent (governor) Miklos Horthy:[2]

> *Dreadful crimes took place, the crimes that primarily endanger the existence of Hungarianhood, our nation's honor and its future. Those crimes lead to the final collapse and loss of international status of Hungary as a state...*
>
> *In the process of occupying Bachka, according to the serious accounts, around 8,500 people, mostly Serbs, were shot... Most of those were innocent people or insignificant transgressors and most of them were women and children. When I visited Novi Sad in early November last year [1941], I listened about those things with deep sadness...*

General Bayor began his tenure with an offensive poster that made equal all the Jews, Gypsies and Serbs... It was unnecessary and harmful to speak in such a manner about the chivalrous and honorable Serbian people of which only a month before the Hungarian public and the press abound with the words of praise... General Bayor did not stop at needless and damaging insults that had nothing in common with the Hungarian soul, but he has, to my recollection, in that harsh poster, called on all the Serbs, Gypsies and Jews who have moved to Novi Sad and the surrounding areas after 1918, to leave the country in three days. Those unfortunates, in my findings about 24,000 persons, had no right to take their movables or anything else other than 30 pengs. They were transferred with infants and children to the other side of Danube to Croatian and Serbian anarchy. In addition, those who remained continued to suffer unnecessary harassment and prosecution. Residence of the Serbian bishop, a man venerable and honored by the entire Europe as a person and scientist, was beleaguered and kept at gun point for days. General Bayor, or his men, collected certain amounts of money from Serbs and Jews, which they represented as taxes and had used as a fund from which the large part, to my knowledge, was used independently...

This year, on January 4, the gendarmerie in Zhabaly* got the report that one of the ranches, for which we believed was unsettled, had a smoking chimney. Hearing this, the captain gathered two dozen armed men, gendarmes, police and border guards in order to raid the farm mentioned above. When they approached it at gun reach, they were welcomed with rifle fire from the farm. Five people were shot, two wounded, while others withdrew. Armed assistance from Szeged and Novi Sad was requested... They surrounded the entire district of Zhabaly, penetrating towards the suspected farm on the river Tisa. When Hungarian troops approached the farm, they met rifle fire as the rebels accepted the fight. Allegedly, four more Hungarian soldiers

---

* Zhabaly is a village in the Shaikashka region near the city of Novi Sad.

ОБЈАВА!

Наређујем градском и општинском становништву, да се приликом претреса и (рација), која ће се извршити од стране војних власти, строго придржава према ниже наведеним наредбама:

1. Приликом претреса приватна својина остаје неповређена. Пријаве о крађи и насиљу на лицу места извршиоцу, а крадљивца стављају под преки суд.

2. Сваки непотребни улични саобраћај забрањујем. По улицама могу слободно кретати само чиновници и радници, који су запослени у градским или државним радионицама и радњама животних намирница. Ови морају да имају код себе одговарајуће легитимације. Остало становништво може да се креће улицама

само између 8 и 18 часова

и то само за извршење најпотребнијих послова (напр. за набавку животних намирница). Стајање и груписање по улицама забрањено је, т. ј. свако групно кретање, забрањено је. По улицама дозвољено је кретање

само пешице, кораком и само средином пута.

3. Само онај може да путује возом, који може да докаже неодложну потребу путовања (напр. смртни случај у породици итд.)

4. У град (општину) нико стран не може ући. Изузетак чине само кола, која преносе средства за огрев, животне намирнице и која су за то добила од града (општине) нарочиту дозволу.

5. Све радње морају бити затворене. Изузетно чине само радње са животним намирницама, које треба да су отворене од 8 до 18 часова.

6. У свакој кући кућевласник (пазикућа), у свакој радњи власник радње или члан његове породице, мора бити властима при руци.

7. Забрањујем сваки аутобуски саобраћај, моторних кола и колски саобраћај, као и свако поштанско уручење.

8. Забрањено је слушати радио.

9. Употреба приватних телефона забрањена је.

10. Забрањено је точење алкохолних пића.

11. Сва места за забављање, као. биоскопи, позоришта, посластичарнице, кафане итд. морају бити затворене. Изузетак чине само ресторације (менза), које могу бити отворене само од 8-12 часова. Задржавање у ресторацијама и мензама, ограничава се само за време обеда.

12. Све цркве, капеле и богомоље морају бити стално затворене. Звоњење је забрањено.

13. Сваки друштвени живот и посећивање клубова забрањено је.

14. Забрањено је свако скупљање друштва — т. ј. и у приватним становима.

15. Преко целога дана прозоре треба држати затворене и са спуштеним завесама.

16. Сва капије од кућа морају бити и дању и ноћу закључане. Они лични који извршују претрес, капија се без одлагања мора одмах отворити. Строго је забрањено страна лица пуштати у кућу.

17. Строго је забрањено страна лица примати (сакривати) у кућу (приватне станове, подруме, тавани, складишта, радње, творнице итд). Такве особе одмах треба предати властима. За то су одговорни: кућевласници, пазикуће, станари ...

18. Свако оружје, муницију, експлозив ... требa предати ... без власти ... поступити према овим ... муницију или експлозив ...

19. ... ће узети на одговор ... који се не буду држали наведених наредбама.

ВОЈНА МЕСНА КОМАНДА

A photo of the announcement informing the citizens of Novi Sad that the Razzia would be carried out January 21-23, 1942.

and gendarmes were killed, but the rebels suffered even greater losses. Fewer rebels fled and even smaller number of those—allegedly five— were captured. Several days later those captured were sentenced to death and executed by a military kangaroo court...according to information received from several directions, it is important that...we can say that the rebellion in Zhabaly was easily crushed from the military standpoint...

According to one version, during the pogrom in Zhabaly the soldiers gathered over the night...the vast majority of Serbs and in small part Jews, the entire families with women, girls, children and infants. They were brought to the bank of the Tisa in military trucks... after which they were gunned down with automatic rifles and then tossed into the Tisa through a hole sliced in the ice. According to another version, this killing took place in Zhabaly in smaller segments from January 5 to January 19. In the neighboring large district of Churug,† this slaughter was allegedly performed from house to house. The residents stood in front of a military truck, in which the corpses were thrown. When the truck would fill with bodies, they were transported to the Tisa and the corpses were thrown under the ice. The truck would then return and in that way unraveled the eerie slaughter in which no mercy was shown to the children or elderly as long as the truck was waiting to be filled...

... Everything that happened at the time was after the removal of the military aspect of the entire issue, and not on the enemies', but on the Hungarian state territory. If the rebels were helped by the women and children, it is perhaps understandable that those were injured or shot. However, if a really small-scale armed rebellion was already liquidated, yet the population of the entire two districts was given over to the mercy of the soldiers, gendarmes and the local National Guard, which had been shooting them for two weeks in a

† Churug is the largest and richest village in the Shaikashka region, located near the city of Novi Sad.

Members of the Hungarian Danube flotilla in Novi Sad, working at a dock on the river.

bloody violence and the most inhumane and unHungarian manner, it is such a terrible mistake and blow to the Hungarian legal system, as well as a dangerous form of civil war that every genuine Hungarian has to speak against... I wrote a letter that was consistent with the seriousness, tragedy of the situation and my elementary arousal. In that letter, I begged and demanded the end to that organized, officially led pogromic chain, and punishment for the culprits. I sent the letter on January 21 to the Prime Minister Laszlo Bardossy. The next day he phoned me personally and asked me to visit him in his apartment. The subject of my letter was not only the Zhabaly pogrom, but also the issue of participation of the Hungarian Home Defense Force in the war against Soviet Russia... He was under the strong impression of my letter the day before, 21st January, so he phoned Novi Sad with order that there be no cruelty... Only much later, when I received a notice about the Novi Sad pogrom, I had come to know that at the time that I had a meeting with the head of the government (as far as I remember, that was January 22), the pogrom in Novi Sad was already underway. I particularly warned the Prime Minister on January 21, sometimes between 2 and 3 p.m., about the massacre in Zhabaly. Thus, he made a telephone call to Novi Sad the very same day—the first day of the pogrom, but his instructions did not produce any effect because a three-day pogrom in Novi Sad got underway and proceeded in its dishonorable progress. Therefore, I certainly must conclude that what happened implies a serious political liability of the Prime Minister in this matter because he cannot say that he was not promptly informed, at least in terms of the Novi Sad pogrom. At that very moment, he had sufficient time and mechanisms to do something. Or, if he had no sufficient power for a specific undertaking, he could have turned to the people above him, or to the upper constitutional factors.

I was unspeakably shocked when I received, after all this, the news about the Novi Sad massacre. I did not want to believe what I heard… the statement by the Prime Minister in my presence that he phoned Novi Sad on January 21 with the order that there be no cruelty, speaks about a serious government commitment. It turns out, however, that Novi Sad pogrom not only surpassed the atrocities, or resembled those crimes in the Shaikashka region, but in its character it was an obvious military pogrom…

On the first day, January 21, using lists of districts, the gendarmes led by NCOs visited homes and legitimized the Serbs and Jews. Then, they were massively transported in military trucks to the river-bank, where groups were stripped naked—male, female and children together—and then shot and thrown in the frozen Danube. Allegedly, the military broke ice with canons during nighttime, so that the water could sweep away the corpses. The number of people shot en masse on the Danube, poorly counting, is several hundreds. But this pogrom did not take place so formalistically because one of my friends from Novi Sad, a respected Hungarian, related to his friends in Budapest that at the Reformation cemetery he saw with his own eyes eighty unburied corpses…they had simplified the work because people were shot in their homes, families with the children were exterminated, houses ransacked, caches burgled, bodies smeared on a military truck and then tossed under the Danube ice.

In several streets, the entire Serbian and Jewish families were exterminated...

Dr. Satler, a Jewish doctor, who treated every poor Hungarian without charge during the Yugoslav government...

Lazarus Manigodich, the secretary of the automobile club... He was shot because they found some mechanic parts in his possession, and accused him that it was probably an explosive device...

Nikolich, a butcher, and his son. On January 20, Hungarian officers visited them. They reportedly said "poor Serbs" before leaving...

Dr. Jovanovich, a pediatrician, who was never involved in politics...

Ivanovich, a journalist, along with his wife who was Hungarian, two brothers, Kon, traders (their money disappeared)...

Cornell Frank, a contractor, together with his spouse and one-year-old child...

I beg Your Highness, on behalf of millions, to punish perpetrators, and if there are barriers, please then put all genuine Hungarians and those of us who have been raising our voice for years in the dock, so that at least in our death we may forget that we were Hungarians. Either this military crime or genuine Hungarians will win. If the former win, then the latter will have to perish...

An official open pogrom without charges, with the exclusion of defense, a mass killing of a great style the history can record in Hungary in January 1942, for the eternal shame...

Every honest Hungarian has to blush. Any beautification and coating would be a huge obstacle to the great cause: the full sentence, the full restitution of the legal system and the fullest possible satisfaction.

...Hungarian soldiers and gendarmes are not there because of mass killing of the honorable and decent citizens, defenseless women, girls, children and infants.

In Novi Sad, for example, the mass murder went on for three days in the official presence of the army commander from Szeged, therefore with his full responsibility. Regarding the killings, robbery and theft that occurred in the city center where only the wealthy individuals lived, I conclude that the excuse for which the Communists there were searched is not good. Should we look for Communists among the wealthy Jewish merchants and educated Serbian intellectuals? Is communism itself a reason to kill with impunity and with no trial—men, women, children and infants?

In Novi Sad, according to the alerts from reliable sources, the following intellectuals and their families were butchered:

Dr. Milosh Bokshan, 65-year-old lawyer and his two sisters; Dr. Pavlas and his wife, Dr. Relya and Dr. Kosta Trifkovich and their mother, wife of Pavle Dobanovachki, as well as her sister; Eng. Zhakich, the director of The Water Supply company and his wife; Eng. Nicholas Dragoylov, son of the Austro-Hungarian admiral...your godson; Milorad Rayich, an authorized bookkeeper after the entering of the Hungarian troops, along with four Serbian priests...every intelligent Hungarian must pose a question: are those truly Communists? What is the benefit of this mass murder, even if they were Communists?

...In Zhabaly, around 1,400 were shot in the Raid, around 3,000 in Churug, in Novi Sad, 2,000-2,500 were shot in the Raid...

Miklos Horthy should not allow his glorious warrior name, the conscience of our nation, the history of his regency, to be tarnished with such filth. Testimonials on all sorts of inhumanity reach heaven and cannot go without punishment...

This memorandum, dated February 4, 1942, states several relevant facts. During the April 1941 occupation about 8,500 Bachka victims were shot. Zhilinsky revealed the data that he possessed at that time. The number of victims in the Novi Sad Razzia accounted for about 2,500 victims, which is already twice more than the post-war Yugoslav claims of approximately 1,246 victims among the Novi Sad citizenry.

THE FIRST DOCUMENT ON THE NOVI SAD RAZZIA

Alarmed by the pogrom, ethnic Germans in Novi Sad immediately invited the German consul in the Hungarian city of Szeged to visit Novi Sad. Consul Kampf's diplomatic report to the German embassy in Budapest on January 31, 1942, is the oldest document on the Novi Sad Razzia. It is housed in the German state military archives (Bundesarchiv-Militar-Archiv), the files of the military intelligence service (Abwehr), file RW 5-Ausland-Abwehr/Ausland VI, v. 476—Jugoslawien.[3] It reads as follows:

HUNGARIAN PENALTIES IN NOVI SAD

Last Saturday, 24th of this month, I had the opportunity on the occasion of a German piano concert to have a word with the local commander of the Corps (Tzaydner) on, as it was reported on 22nd of this month—the number XII/59—briefly reported, Hungarian measures against the Serbian rebels. The general indicated to me that the harsh measures had been taken; it was necessary to perform a large number of executions, but now again peace has been established.

On the 28th of this month, I was informed by Mr. Hans Prohaska, celenlaiter of The Nazi Party in Novi Sad, that I was urgently asked by the Reich Germans in Novi Sad to go there as soon as possible. They were concerned about possible further executions. However, not a single German from the Reich suffered so far, but still, it had to be counted with expecting the unpredictable in case the Serbs renewed their insidious attacks. I calmed Mr. Prohaska. Through him I called on the Reich Germans to preserve peace under any circumstances and announced my possible arrival the following day at noon. I sent a brief telephone message about this at the Legation.

That very afternoon, I looked for the local corps commander and spoke to him about the measures that would be necessary for the special protection of the Reich Germans. The general declared he was willing for that because it is also—which he specifically mentioned—expected the possibility of further rebellion of the Serbs and Communists. In that case, he said, we would strike even tougher and he would therefore take the Reich Germans to a timely protection as much as he is able to. Then he allowed the Colonel Grashy in, the Commander of Novi Sad, who came to file a report. Together we discussed the appropriate measures, and my proposal was that all the Reich Germans would get special passes in Hungarian that would contain a photograph of the holder and would underline that the owner is protected by Honveds. That was immediately accepted.

The following morning, accompanied by a consular officer who previously was a driver for many years, I tried to get to Novi Sad by my car.

Ten kilometers from Szeged, I rushed into a snowdrift. Peasants had to pull me out and five hours later, I was back in Szeged. Finally, I took the only possible transportation, a passenger train to Novi Sad. It took me eight hours to get there. I arrived at night in Novi Sad, so the meeting with the German colony had to be canceled.

The following summary of the situation was presented to me by Mr. Prohaska and other Reich Germans whom I met yesterday early in the morning at the hotel.

Specifically, on the 21st of this month the Hungarian gendarmerie, in cooperation with the army, searched the apartments and began arrests. The first shooting occurred which was not significantly intensified the next day. The number of those affected by these measures was low at that moment… On 23rd…the hundreds of executions occurred… Those that were previously suspicious, known as leading Serbs or Communists, those running away, or those who did not immediately pull out hands from pockets to a call, were shot on the spot. Also, women and children were not spared. Three women, former German citizens, one married to a Jew and the other two to Serbs, were executed in their homes at the side of their husbands. Also, thirteen Russian immigrants, members of Wrangel's army, I have a list of their names, were shot along with their relatives. In total, over 3,000 people, including 800 Jews, have been executed. An exact repeated crosscheck of that figure is not possible at this time. Even before my departure from Szeged, the corps commander, and then in Novi Sad, the Hungarian staff officers, recognized around 2,300 executed, of whom 800 were Jews. That must be the number of dead, but in fact it is much higher. The entire households, especially villas and summerhouses inhabited by the Jews, are empty because every one of their residents is dead.

Reich Germans who saw these events, partly in front of their homes, partly on their way to stores or on the ice of the Danube River, are understandably upset. Serbs, who were their homeowners, work colleagues or acquaintances, lay in the streets, on home porches and elsewhere, and were suddenly dead. It touched the Germans in a painful manner...

A view of elite Mileticheva Street in Novi Sad. The residents of this street were thought to be of noble bearing and intelligence, and were primarily of Serbian and Jewish origin. Most were murdered in the Novi Sad Razzia.

The oldest document written by a neutral diplomat recognizes that high-ranking military leaders of the Hungarian occupying army admitted "around 2,300 executed," but Kampf noted above that the death toll was much higher. The Holocaust Memorial Museum in Washington, in the *Holocaust Encyclopedia*, states, "In January 1942, the Hungarian military units shot 3,000 Jews and Serbs of Novi Sad, the capital of the Yugoslav territory that was annexed by Hungary."[4]

Indications of the number of slain victims of the Novi Sad Razzia appear in the memorandum by Zhilinsky, memoirs written by Dr. Andrew Deak, the newspaper *Free Vojvodina*, and the facts presented in the oldest document on the Novi Sad Razzia— a statement by the German consul Kampf. Moreover, the Hungarian department for national minorities recorded 8,000–10,000 executed victims in "the Shaikashka and Novi Sad raids."[5] A Serbian author, Vasa Kazimirovich, who writes about the cruelty that was applied when "about ten thousand men, women and children were shot," confirms this fact.

The Holocaust Memorial Center in Budapest displays an official exhibit in Hungarian and English about the Novi Sad massacre. The specified number of Jews executed—as displayed on the exhibit itself—is incorrect. Nevertheless, it reveals that under the pretext of fighting against the "partisans," the Hungarian gendarmerie and army in January 1942 organized the bloodshed in Novi Sad. It says that nearly 3,300 innocent people were shot (2,600 Serbs and 700 Jews). Among the slain "partisans" were 729 women and 147 children. Even the Hungarian regent, Miklos Horthy, patron and organizer of the Razzia of 1942, wrote in his memoirs that the official number of Novi Sad victims was 3,309.

The head of the German security police, SS Colonel Minberg, reported on February 25, 1942, to the Ministry of Foreign Affairs in Berlin, of the situation in Bachka, based on the statements by the Hungarian government officials. Minberg noted that in Novi Sad 1,800 Serbs, including women and children, were shot. If eradicated Serbian families in Novi Sad consisted, on average, of at least three members, we understand the statement in the film *Monument*, whose main character was told by his mother that his father was thrown under the ice of the Danube with more than 5,000 men, women, and children. When we add the 1,401 identified Novi Sad Jewish victims, and those of other ethnic origins, of whom there is not a single word in Minberg's report, we remain amazed at the scale of the genocide committed in Novi Sad in January 1942.

SWEDISH PRESS REPORTS JANUARY 1942 GENOCIDE

The following text is a translation from an article published in the Swedish newspaper *Socialdemocrat* on October 12, 1943. The article, titled, "Hungarian Massacre of 10,000 Serbs," describes the genocide taking place in Hungary.

Hungarian Massacre of 10,000 Serbs

Responsibility now assigned to Nazi Officer
Brave Social Democratic Protests Against this Horrific Deed

By the Social Democrat's Foreign Correspondent, Nils Horney

BUDAPEST, October 1943

Hungarian treatment of Jews and the population of occupied areas have blemishes that will not be easy to wash away. One is the massacre of 10,000 Jews and Serbians in the winter of 1942 in the Bachka Region. The other is the treatment of Jewish worker battalions sent with Hungarian soldiers to the Eastern Front. But despite the Jewish Camps that have been introduced in Hungary, primarily under German pressure, the situation of 800,000 Jews is decent compared to that of Jews in Germany, Romania and Slovakia, where the extermination of Jews is suffering from a lack of available victims. Hungarian officials are resisting German pressure to implement a similar extermination program.

The article then continues to discuss atrocities against Jews in Russia and elsewhere, including a gruesome depiction of executions and mass burials in which living bodies in a large open grave in the Katyn forest are still moving under a thin blanket of dirt, and boxcars of Jews left on side tracks until all sounds of life are gone from the frozen and trampled bodies inside, while assigning blame to "Nazi-leaning Hungarian officers impressed by German methods." The Swedish article resumes:

The same can be said of the mass murder in the winter of 1942 in the Bachka region of southern Hungary, which for hundreds of years, until the end of WWI, had been primarily a Serbian-populated area, until after the collapse of Yugoslavia became occupied by Hungarian troops.

Social-Democratic Leader Protests in Parliament

According to a member-in-exile of Yugoslavia's government, in a Swedish propaganda brochure, not less than 16,000 Jews and Serbians were massacred in the Bachka region in the winter of 1942. In my experience in the Balkan region, tales of grisly deeds are often exaggerated beyond recognition, even if there is usually an extremely large grain of truth behind the inflated tales. I have sought to verify the Yugoslavian reports in Hungary and have found them largely validated. When the massacres became known in Budapest, the Social-democratic leader, Karoly Peyer, and one of the Farmers Party leaders led a discussion in the Foreign Affairs Committee, a brave action, considering the repercussions that could have occurred, and may yet occur, as German-influence is increasingly felt in Hungary. The repercussions against Karoly [sic] Peyer seem to have been limited to Prime Minister Kallay's expression of disapproval over his action by removing him from the Foreign Affairs Committee. The government sought to keep the matter secret, without success. Stories about what happened in Bachka spread to the outside world, and on July 15th Milan Popovics initiated a Parliamentary procedure in the lower house about the measures the government took in

smala fjordar, som äro spärrade av minfält och u-båtsfällor och ständigt bevakade av vakt-fartyg.

*T*ysk förstörelse på östfronten: Järnvägarna sprängas och rälsen förstöres för att hindra tysk framryckning.

i London förklarar man att enda möjligh tuella fredstrevare tagna i betraktande via anaraat och direkt söka kontakt med Moskv

Se vidare sidorna 6

Ungersk massaker på 10,000 serber

Ansvaret lägges nu på nazistofficerare

Modig socialdemokratisk protest mot det ohyggliga dådet.

Från Social-Demokratens utsände medarbetare
NILS HORNEY.

BUDAPEST I oktober.
Den ungerska behandlingen av judar och av befolkningen i ocku-perade områden har ett par allvarliga skönhetsfläckar som inte bli lätta att tvätta bort: Den ena är massakrerna i det serbiska Bacska-området vintern 1942, då sammanlagt 10,000 serber och judar mör-dades. Den andra är behandlingen av de judiska arbetsbataljoner som sänts med de ungerska trupperna till östfronten. Men trots de judelagar som huvudsakligen under tysk påtryckning införts i Ungern är de 800,000 ungerska judarnas ställning dräglig, jämförd med för-hållandena i Tyskland, Rumänien och Slovakien, där utrotningskriget mot judarna nu lider mot sitt slut av brist på fler offer. De ansva-riga ungerska myndigheterna ha vägrat att efterkomma tyska krav på ett sådant utrotningskrig.

Fortsättning på sista sidan.

Statsministern Kallay.

Dödsskott vid älgjakt
Se olyckskrönikan sista sidan.

Svensk ångare sänkt i Gdynia

Angfartyget A. K. Fernström av Karlshamn har i dagarna förolyckats i Gdynias hamn enligt tele-grem till utrikesdepartementet från svenska konsulatet i Danzig. Be-sättningen, som uppgick till 14 man, är oskadad och kommer att hemsändas till Sverige. Det för-modas att fartyget träffats vid flyg-anfall mot Gdynia.

Arbetets Värmlan

Roquefortost och vär₁

Tre män singlade ned från rymden

All Värr form inbju gens skapa

Photo of the Swedish article published in the newspaper Socialdemocrat on October 12, 1943.

reaction to the event. Apparently the procedure was conducted with the consent of Prime Minister Kallay. Popovics, who had been the leader of an anti-Bolshevik Serbian organization in Belgrade, was made lower-house representative of the re-conquered Serbian region and is therefore not the Serbian population's elected representative. Kallay was also immediately ready to answer the procedure. He explained that an investigation had been made and presented that from the German-occupied Banat, an area partially populated by Serbs, previously occupied by Hungary, Serbian Communist "free troops" pushed into Bachka and initiated a guerilla war against the Serbian police force. The Prime Minister submitted that these free forces were protected by the indigenous population but contradicted himself by explaining that 'Bachka is a quiet and peaceful region in which foreigners wish to cause a disturbance' and that 'neither the

Hungarian authorities nor the local Serbs were responsible for that which happened.' Kallay explained further that 2,550 Serbs had been killed, including 292 in Ujvidek [the Hungarian name for Novi Sad]. He lamented that the Hungarian military which had been called in to squelch an uprising with the 'character of an open revolt' had been 'too zealous' and exceeded its authority with the result that innocent people had lost their lives. Legal action had been taken against some of the leaders for this military campaign.

The Official Version is a Cover-Up

In Hungary, I have received information from persons who stayed in Ujvidek during the massacre and who themselves almost fell victims to it that show the official Hungarian version of the event to be an orchestrated cover-up. While Prime Minister Kallay stated that 2,550 Serbians were killed, and from the direction of Yugoslavia we are informed that 16,000 sacrificed their lives, my informants maintain the number of dead in Bachka to be "at least 10,000". According to the Yugoslavian information in Ujvidek alone, 1,892 people were murdered. My informants believe the number was at least that number. And they explain it was not "Communists", or agitators who were murdered, unless by rare coincidence. Most of the victims in Ujvidek were Jews living in the town. Almost all of the Jews and educated Serbs were murdered. Women and children were not spared. The population was forced to stay indoors, while the houses were searched and 'the guilty' were led to the Danube, forced into groups and mowed down with volleys of bullets, after which the corpses were tossed into holes in the ice. Just about every detail from my informants agrees with those delivered from Serbia. That the Hungarian troops were 'too zealous' was due to, among other things, that Hungarian party leaders in Ujvidek mistakenly forced a few Hungarian civil servants and Germans living in town onto the icy river and shot them down. I've seen supporting documentation on this from official Hungarian sources.

The mass slaughter in Ujvidek began on the 21st of January and continued for three days. According to Prime Minister Kallay's own testimony in his hearing, the town was 'completely calm, at least during the first two days, while a portion of the population, on the third day, tried to resist, in obvious desperation'.

The General was decorated—and sentenced to two years in jail.

According to what was delivered to me, the authorities in Budapest were informed as to what was taking place in Ujvidek already on day one. Not until the third day did the central authorities intervene. Otherwise the massacre would likely have continued. General Ferencz Bayer, who had command over the troops, was apparently first decorated for the 'resourcefulness' he displayed. When the actual circumstances became evident and a violent indignation arose in the Hungarian parliament, over time, legal action was taken and the general was sentenced to two years in jail. I was told by official sources that other officers who participated in the massacre could not be brought before the court because they had been moved with their unit to the Eastern Front. The general opinion in Hungary is meanwhile not at peace that offenders have so easily gotten away and demand that a new, thorough investigation be held, with punishments which, by some reasonable measure, fit the crimes. Such a readjustment is a minimum requirement, if Hungary is to retain its reputation as a civilized nation, argued the opposition.

Officially I have been told that General Bayer and other Nazi-influenced officers carried out the massacres in Bachka without authorization from higher sources. They designate the general's behavior as clear sabotage of Hungarian interests with the intent to promote German efforts to divide and conquer, as illustrated in the Balkans and elsewhere. Hungary's politics during the years between the two world wars have been focused on friendly relations with Yugoslavia. Just months prior to Germany's attack on Yugoslavia, the Hungarian and Yugoslavian governments entered into a friendship pact. And three days before the German attack on Yugoslavia, Hungary's Prime Minister at the time, the patriotic but warm-hearted and humanitarian Count Paul Teleki, committed suicide in protest against what he knew was about to happen. For decades he had worked as a scientist and statesman for a peaceful way to undo, from a Hungarian perspective, the hard and unjust Treaty of Trianon. He foresaw that Hungary would be drawn into a Witch's Sabbath of hate and thirst for revenge, which, in the long run, would be damaging to the nation. Through his death he sought to awaken the country's reflection and conscience.

He didn't sacrifice himself in vain. Opposition to Hungary being drawn into the war has grown stronger, and has, in a way that honors Hungary, turned against the German-influenced military violence.

DECEPTIONS ABOUT THE NUMBER OF RAZZIA 1942 VICTIMS IN SERBIAN HISTORY

A t least 45 Novi Sad victims were murdered on January 21, 1942. At least 48 victims were shot on January 22, and an unknown number during that night.[1] On January 23, 1942, a massive war crime was committed by Hungarian occupiers. On that day, many people were executed in the streets and in their homes. From the morning until about 3 p.m., the citizens of Novi Sad were forcibly taken to municipal Strand Beach. Around noon, Dr. Andrew Deak and his family were driven to that most beautiful European river beach. In front of them were about 2,000 people lined in the column of death. When the slaughter of Serbs and Jews stopped, all the people in the line were exterminated to the last, to which Dr. Deak testified in his extraordinary memoirs.[2]

The oldest newspaper article about the number of Novi Sad Razzia victims was published in *Free Voyvodina* in January 1944. It states, "Three thousand disfigured, naked and robbed corpses of Novi Sad citizens were received by the cold Danube waves."[3]

In 1984, the Institute for History published a book entitled *Children of the Rebellious Plain*, whose author writes, "According to incomplete data provided by the Investigation Commission following the war, an identity of 1,040 victims has been established." However, several authors who have studied those bloody events have written in their works that around 2,000 Novi Sad citizens were deprived of their lives. Nevertheless, according to recent data, which is now considered to be the most accurate approximate number, 3,309 Serbs and Jews in Novi Sad were executed, including 144 children. Even these figures cannot be considered as the final say on the issue.[4]

Aranka Stoyanovich, nee Hayosh, and her daughter from her first marriage, Dorothea Pintar, some years before their deaths in Razzia. Six members of the Hayosh family were taken on January 23, 1942, from their home in Novi Sad, driven to the city river beach and murdered.

Not even those figures—at that time the most precise—were complete. The Regional Commission for Investigation of Crimes Committed by the Occupiers and Their Collaborators in Vojvodina confirmed that the exact number of the victims had not been presented to the public due to lack of data. The Commission gave no indication about the number of the victims whose identities had not been established. That official post-war data about Novi Sad residents eradicated in the Razzia dates back to 1947. The former Yugoslavia state authorities established the identity of 1,040 murdered Serbs and Jews in Bachka from the day of Hungarian occupation up to June 19, 1944. Bearing in mind multiple failures in the method of data collecting, recording and processing, that report by the socialist Yugoslavia cannot be considered a credible source. The author of the monograph about painter Bogdan Shuput, who is a victim of the Novi Sad Razzia, wrote the following in 1984:

According to the official information, the Hungarian occupation forces shot in total 879 Novi Sad residents between January 20 and January 23, 1942. According to unofficial information, 3,000-5,000 were murdered. Several sources claim around 2,000 victims. Based

A photo of victims shot at the Serbian Orthodox cemetery in Novi Sad on January 23, 1942.

on incomplete information, the Investigation Commission established 1,040 Novi Sad Razzia victims. Figures vary to such an extent that it will probably be impossible to determine the truth. No doubt the truth is even more brutal.[5]

The Regional Commission published its established numbers of murdered victims from all the villages and towns in Shaikashka where the Razzia of 1942 was committed. In the study of the crimes committed against the Jews, the Commission writes:

Hungarian gendarmerie in Churug shot to the last man all 100 Jews who lived there in January 1942… In Novi Sad entire Jewish families were exterminated. The total number of Jews murdered in Novi Sad is 870 (Inv. No. 4977).[6]

The data presented by the Regional Commission are "neither complete, nor always accurate." Besides, it received information only from

Seen from a distance are those about to be shot, waiting by the Novi Sad Strand.

those who came in to register their relatives (not every single victim). This is quite obvious in the example of the village of Nadaly. The record is incomplete as to all the categories of the circumstances under which the victims from that village lost their lives at the hands of Horthy's murderers. The record about Nadaly victims is faulty because "it is well-known that the number of all the victims from Nadaly is much higher," writes the author of the Nadaly chronicle.[7]

In 1960, the Serbian *Journal for Social Science*, No. 27, published an article written by Zhivan Kumanov, "Bachka in the National Liberation War: a Brief Review" containing the following statement:

A portrait of Andrew Havash, a Novi Sad Razzia victim. The photo was taken during Hannukah 1941, just prior to his murder in the Razzia of January 1942.

The Razzia was performed in Novi Sad on January 21-23. Over 2,000 people were murdered.[8]

Nine years later, George Vasich wrote that the Hungarian occupiers had undertaken "a couple of the historically dirtiest and the most bestial military and police actions—raids in Shaikashka and Novi Sad." Vasich cited the statement of the Regional Commission that in Novi Sad 1,043 people were murdered, as well as the report of the occupying forces that stated 879 people were shot: 292 Serbs, 556 Jews, thirteen Russians, eight Hungarians, seven Germans, two Croats and one Slovak (418 men, 322 women, fifty-three children and eighty-six elderly).[9]

In 1970, George Labovich and Peter Razhnatovich wrote a text, *The Slaughter on Danube Banks*, without clearly defining the figures:

In the Novi Sad January massacre, thousands of Serbs, Jews, and genuine Novi Sad patriots were murdered.[10]

In 1974, Milorad Tchurchin published a work on the "raids" carried out in the Shaikashka villages surrounding the city of Novi Sad. In his book, 593 victims are recorded in the village of Zhabaly, 864 in the village of Churug, 81 in the village of Gospodyinci, and 210 in the village of Gyurgyevo. Tchurchin immediately distances himself from these data:

Surely these data are not completely accurate because there was no one to report on many victims, since certain families were completely destroyed and no one was left behind who could have registered them.[11]

It is that crucial recognition which has been avoided for eight decades in postwar historiography. In Novi Sad, there was also no one to register many victims. That is what the German consul alluded to when he wrote that many homes remained desolate and the number of victims must be certainly much higher compared to the figure that Hungarian officers admitted to him. Moreover, the "raid" was launched on the Serbian St. John's Day, when various guests from other places visited relatives and friends who celebrated that feast in Novi Sad. Who could have known the identity of eighteen guests who came to the Mashin house? Who registered and numbered the Roma individuals from Rakovachka Street, where Hungarian Nazi gendarmes came and shot some on the very street, while others were piled into a truck and driven to Strand Beach? It was never said of the people who came to Novi Sad how many were taken from the train station right to the murder site! The identity of the majority of Jewish immigrants who found refuge in Novi Sad from German-occupied countries in Europe is not known, only that there were about 300 such individuals. Unknown are the identities of fifty prisoners who were taken from the torture prison in Novi Sad and thrown under the ice!

With these facts in mind, we must certainly draw a conclusion that, in the case of many victims, no one remained to report their deaths. Since their identities remain unknown, this does not mean that they are (what an absurdity of the modern falsified Serbian history!) fewer in number, but quite the contrary.

In 1975, Laza M. Kostich, a lawyer with a PhD in statistics, published a book, *Serbs and Hungarians in the XIX and XX Century*, about the "raids" in Shaikashka and Novi Sad. He wrote:

> *The order to halt the raids came from Budapest before all the Serbs were cleansed from those regions, yet after several thousand Serbs had already been shot and thrown into the Danube. The numbers diverge: the Serbs claim 30,000 dead, while Hungarians admit barely a tenth part of that number. I think that, regardless of the Jewish and Gypsy victims, about 10,000 Serbs were shot, who had no fault other than being of Serbian origin.*[12]

The established falsified assertion on the number of victims appeared in 1978 in the book *Yugoslavia: Before and During World War II*:

> *The killing of Novi Sad Serbs occurred in January 1942. Miklos Horthy also mentioned that event in his Memoirs. Horthy says, "Many innocent persons were shot and thrown into the Danube. The number of Jewish, Serbian and Hungarian victims was later estimated to 1,300 persons."*[13]

Horthy was preparing a speech to be delivered on March 15, 1944, which he did not manage to give. In that speech, there is a clause quoted by the Hungarian writer Janosh Buzashy in his book *Novi Sad Razzia*, "All of us condemn the Novi Sad incidents because on that occasion around 3,000 people lost their lives."[14]

Former president of the Novi Sad Jewish community, Paul Shosberger (now deceased), notes that the "raid" was actually a hunt for Jews and Serbs. He claims that 870 Novi Sad Jews were shot, yet has identified only 827 in one of his books.[15]

In 1980, the Jewish historian Jasha Romano described the various forms of the Holocaust that took place in the Balkans during the Second World War. He pointed out that 323 Jews were shot in the January 1942 genocide in the Shaikashka region, while in Novi Sad "the most bestial murders" took place claiming the lives of "789 Jews and several thousand Serbs."[16]

In 1984, the Institute for History based in Novi Sad published *Vojvodina in the Liberation War and Socialist Revolution 1941-1945*, which states that "the genocidal operation, known as the 'Razzia' claimed the lives of 2,260 people in Shaikashka and 206 in the town of Bechey." As far as the Novi Sad Razzia is concerned, the author writes that "in January 21-23, around 2,000 people—Jews and Serbs—were slaughtered and thrown under the ice of Danube."[17]

In his book *Games on the Danube*, author Ivan Ivanyi recalls this memory from childhood:

> *A half year later, in January 1942, six thousand people were killed right on this beach on the Danube. I can remember the date so precisely because I turned thirteen the next day.*[18]

The climax of inconsistencies in media and literary reports about Novi Sad Razzia victims appeared in 2006, when Dr. Ephraim Zuroff from the Simon Wiesenthal Center discovered a perpetrator of the Novi Sad pogrom, Sandor Kepiro. The Hungarian news agency MTI reported that 1,250 Jews were liquidated in the Novi Sad Great Raid. The number of victims of other nationalities was not announced.[19]

THE TURNING POINT IN MEDIA COVERAGE

After many decades of misinformation regarding the extent of the Razzia, Novi Sad journalist Igor Mihalyevich made a historic break with forgeries on September 12, 2007, in his article in the regional newspaper, *Daily News* (*Dnevnik*):

We must remember that Kepiro is known to be a Nazi Hungarian gen-
darmerie officer who participated in the January Razzia of 1942. He
was one of the three chief operative personnel in what would become the
bloodiest event in the history of Novi Sad, the genocide, when the ice of
Danube received thousands of citizens, mostly Jews, Serbs and Roma.

For the first time in Serbian history, genuine figures and facts were published about the terrible event in 1942: the fact that the number of victims
is several thousand and that the Novi Sad Razzia was no less than genocide!

THE OLDEST SERBIAN DOCUMENT ABOUT THE RAZZIA OF 1942

"Serbs in 'Southern Hungary,'" an unsigned intelligence report, is the
oldest Serbian testimony about the number of executed victims during the Razzia, written in 1942 by a follower of Drazha Mihailovich. It
emphasizes the fact that the Razzia in Novi Sad was carried out systematically. The document does not provide even an approximate number of
Novi Sad victims; it lists only fifty-eight names, with notices about the
number of members in each listed family who were shot.

There is no sufficient data for members of all ethnic groups who
perished in the Razzia. Shortly after the crime, estimates of the number
of murdered citizens appeared. A resistance hero, Svetozar Toza Markovich,
wrote a report to partisans on May 20, 1942, in which he says that in
the Novi Sad Razzia "more than 2,000 people paid with their lives." A
few months later, on October 10, Branko Bayich and Toza Markovich
wrote another report saying that "around 10,000 souls" were shot in all
the Shaikashka villages and the city of Novi Sad.[20]

The exact number of the victims shot in the Novi Sad Razzia has
never been established, as testified by the Regional Commission:

Partial list of victims is presented, since a complete list of the Jews shot
during Razzia cannot be compiled due to insufficient data.[21]

A poster designed by producer Ivan Kalauzovic. He designed it because a Hungarian court released Sandor Kepiro, who had been indicted for war crimes in Novi Sad, on July 18, 2011. Kepiro died on September 3, 2011.

*Novi Sad, July 24, 2011, a public protest on the occasion of the acquittal of Sandor Kepiro,
the commanding gendarme of the Novi Sad Razzia.*

The former president of the Jewish community in Novi Sad,
Vladislav Rotbart (now deceased), wrote in his work about the prisons
and concentration camps of Horthy's Hungary for the residents of the
occupied parts of Serbia and former Yugoslavia, that around 2,000 Jews
were murdered in colonies where the Razzia was carried out.[22] So far
a total of 1,831 Jewish victims of the Razzia have been identified by
name. However, around 300 Jewish refugees from other parts of Europe
also resided in Novi Sad. They escaped persecution in the lands occupied by Nazi Germany prior to its attack on former Yugoslavia. Having
no proper documents of residence meant that their fate was sealed in
the Razzia. The identity of those emigrant Jews has remained largely
unknown. Thus, it is true that around 2,000 Jews were murdered in cold
blood in Razzia.

So far, 410 victims of non-Serbian and non-Jewish origin have been identified. Unfortunately, 150 Slovak Razzia victims from Kisach village remain unidentified by name. At the same time, only 90 Roma victims have been identified by name, yet there are indications that their number is far greater.

Comparing all the known data about the number of Razzia 1942 victims, it turns out that the claims of the Hungarian deputy Endre Baichy Zhilinsky have withstood the test of veracity beyond a shadow of a doubt. Namely, Swedish journalist Nils Horney claims that over 10,000 Serbs were murdered. The Jewish sources claim around 2,000 Jewish victims. Among victims of other origin, 410 have been identified by name, with indications that their number is far greater. All those figures total 12,763. Therefore, the veracity of the figures coming from the Hungarian sources has proved to be correct.[23]

WITNESS ACCOUNTS

3

In any investigation, the witness statements play a crucial role in identifying and assessing the facts. Such is the case regarding the number of Novi Sad Razzia victims. So far, this author has identified only 2,370 victims.

A QUOTE FROM A WAR JOURNAL

The earliest record of the number of Razzia victims in Novi Sad is found in Vladimir Popovich's diary. His journal was typed out after the war. In the entry dated March 15, 1942, there is the following statement:

> *On January 22 and 23, a horrible massacre of the Serbs took place in the city. Holes were created in several locations on the icy Danube, the citizens were brought to the holes; they were stripped, shot and thrown into the water...several thousand men, women and children.*[1]

A FILM ABOUT THE NOVI SAD RAZZIA

In 1967, a famous Serbian poet, Miroslav Antich, made a movie about the Novi Sad Razzia. The mother of the main character in the film tells her son that in 1942, more than 5,000 men, women, and children in Novi Sad were tossed under the Danube ice. The son intended to marry an ethnic Hungarian girl.

This bold film, *Monument*, sharply criticized the postwar injustice to the victims due to the absence of a monument to their honor. It is a wonder that the Yugoslav communist regime of that time allowed such a rare piece of art to go public. In 1971, a monument in Novi Sad was erected. The spot where it was erected, however, was not the true site on which the majority of mass murders of the Razzia took place—Novi Sad's Strand Beach. A kilometer away, on the banks of the Danube, a place for the monument was chosen "for the sake of tourist attraction." The monument had been waiting for adoption for quite some time. Its creator offered it in 1956 to the Serbian city of Kragujevac and was rejected. He kept offering his piece of art to different cities until Novi Sad authorities accepted it as a "gift" from the artist.

The film *Monument* was an avant-garde film made to preserve the memory of the victims. It seems to have achieved its primary goal. A monument was erected, albeit not inspired by the Razzia of 1942. It was a general monument to all Novi Sad Second World War victims! Thus, the purpose of the monument which stands to this day in Novi Sad was to allay public concerns and lull the citizens into complete oblivion of the essence of the Hungarian Nazi Razzia: the diminished number of victims and the brutal methods by which they were exterminated! Witness Tosha Slankamenatz, who lost twenty-two family members during the Novi Sad Razzia, states in the film that he heard that "in that big slaughter over 4,000 Novi Sad citizens were shot."[2]

RADIO DRAMA BANNED IN 1986

The film produced by Miroslav Antich was spared from censorship probably because it was attributed to poetic freedom and because the main characters were portrayed as members of the Communist party. Twenty years later the artistic freedom regarding the Razzia was suspended. The main reason for that was the fact that witnesses who survived the Genocide stated the exact figures. As if they sensed the fate of their radio drama, the authors concluded the program by saying that they did not want silent memorial plates (by the monument on the Danube banks), but living testimonies.

The Yugoslav festival of radio dramas of 1986, in the Macedonian capital Skopje, pronounced the documentary radio drama produced by Radio Novi Sad the best. However, that radio program was immediately removed under the pretext that "relations between various nationalities in Yugoslavia should not be disturbed." The radio work was kept in darkness for a decade before the Ecological Movement of Novi Sad brought it to light with the permission of the authors. The last witness to speak in the broadcast was Zharko Vuyich, who said that those who survived the massacre in Novi Sad went out to the streets on January 24, 1942. They found hairpins, combs, and frozen blood in the ice. Vuyich ends his testimony saying that the Razzia was over, "yet thousands of Novi Sad citizens remained in the frozen ground and frozen Danube."[3]

VICTIMS "OMITTED" IN THE REGISTRATION PROCESS

4

Doctor Strasser

The testimony of a Novi Sad refugee given in Belgrade, in March 1943, describes several Razzia events and victims. The former municipal clerk testified about the victims not published in any written source, such as the dentist George Strasser.[1] That document is proof that there has never been a systematic work of collecting the relevant data in the field, nor was there a proper processing of data that could have led to identification of more Novi Sad Razzia victims.

The Victim from Sremska Kamenica

More evidence to support that a comprehensive survey of the victims has never been conducted is the case of Dragitza Marich, originally from Sremska Kamenica, a settlement across the Danube from Novi Sad. She is included in the list of fascism victims in a book dedicated to Second World War events in Sremska Kamenica.[2] Dragitza has never been officially registered as a victim of the Novi Sad Razzia 1942.

The Honorable Officer

"Gentlemen, something is not right here. I gave my oath solely to one King and one Homeland," replied Janos Sabo to Hungarian Nazis who invited him to join them in the killing spree in Novi Sad. He alluded to the Serbian king and the Serbian homeland. Because of his officer's honor, Sabo was thrown under the ice. The written documents about this hero do not exist, so he would have remained another secret of the "city under the ice" had the truth about his fate not been discreetly transferred from generation to generation within his family.

Sabo's sister never wanted to talk about her brother. Before she passed away, she confided to her son the truth about the honor and withstanding of a true royal officer. At the end of his life, Sabo's nephew entrusted his daughter with those details. For fifteen years, the cherished secret was kept from the public after Sabo's nephew died. Any new knowledge about the cruel way the victims were deprived of their lives renewed the awareness of Sabo's great niece that the "raid" should be analyzed from all angles. She first bestowed the secret to those in whom she had most confidence, and later to TV viewers in the most accurate documentary program that has ever been produced on the subject of the January 1942 Razzia.[3]

A photo of Rabbi Otto Deutch with Hermina, his wife. Hermina was rescued by Bulgarian tradesmen who smuggled her and her son out of Novi Sad to Italy. The rabbi was found by the occupying gendarmes, who stripped him naked. When they saw that he was circumcised, they took him to the murder site Strand, shot him, and threw him into the Danube.

In January 2009, another fact was revealed that had been concealed for seven long decades. Another unidentified victim received his name. When he swore allegiance to the king, the thought did not even cross Janos Sabo's mind that the icy Danube in January 1942 would be the final test of his great honor.

The Forgotten Rabbi

Identical to Dragitza Marich's case is that of Otto Deutch. The example of Rabbi Deutch also demonstrates the absence of a coordinated approach to collecting data on the victims of the January 1942 genocide. In fact, there were deliberate attempts to cover up a large number of victims. At Louise Stayich's home in Novi Sad, a photo of her childhood friend Hermina, and her husband, Otto Deutch, had stood on a shelf for decades. Louise Stayich, interviewed by one of the best journalists in Novi Sad, has rescued another victim from oblivion.[4]

The Morgenstern Family

Anna Morgenstern, *nee* Mandelbaum, was shot during the Novi Sad Razzia. That is all the data contained on her card at the regional museum. Her maiden name automatically raised questions about other members of her family. For many years, there was no answer to that mystery due to the intricacies caused by diverse testimonies from relatives, friends, and acquaintances kept in the Yad Vashem database of Holocaust victims. In April 2010, I felt a sudden urge to tackle again the "Morgenstern dilemma" and research all the aspects of various written testimonies on their fate. When I clarified all the unknowns, the icy Danube tomb revealed another secret—a five-member Jewish family!

After the Nazi rise to power in Germany, the Morgensterns were deported from Dresden to the Ukrainian birthplace of Anna Morgenstern and her husband, Lvov. Did they come to Novi Sad, where several Morgensterns (probably their relatives) lived, by using their German passports? Or did they flee the Lvov Jewish ghetto which was closed following the German Nazi occupation of Ukraine?

School Memories

Even after several decades, the school memories come to life. Thanks to these, Trudi Pisker and her mother, Julie, who lived nearby the Jewish cultural center in Novi Sad, have been identified as Razzia victims.

Trudi's school friend Leah Wasserman also remembered that the painter Ladislav Shenberger, in addition to a couple of sons, had a daughter, Myra, who is nowhere mentioned in the written sources about victims.[5]

Another memory of school days also clarified the fate of Martha Shimon. Late Leah Lyubibratich narrated about her personal fate and surviving the Razzia 1942, persecutions, and pogroms:

> I went to Serbian high school at the time… I was admitted to that school with the help of Dad's friends, the Serbs, because only three Jewish girls were accepted: Myra Crouse, Martha Shimon, and myself. In the second grade, Martha Shimon's life ended under the ice, thus only Myra and I remained at the school as Jewish girls.[6]

The Fate of Tosha Isakov of Novi Sad

Brothers Tosha and Lazarus lived on Aleksa Shantich Street. Right after the occupation, in April 1941, Horthy's Nazis shot Tosha's brother, the co-owner of a restaurant. Across the street there was a pit with a wall right next to the Isakov house. Lazarus was shot against that wall.

During the January 1942 Razzia, certain citizens were imprisoned in a torture chamber. The written sources mention that on several occasions the Hungarian Nazis took the prisoners to the execution site. We do not have the exact number and identity of those victims, but we know that one of those was Tosha Isakov. His corpse floated out, or was left to float along the bank after it was thrown into the Danube. His niece recognized his coat and clothing. She buried him next to his brother, Lazarus, according to the testimony of Lazarus Isakov Junior.[7]

"WE DO NOT WANT SILENT MEMORIAL PLATES!"

The few examples above vividly illustrate that Novi Sad Razzia victims, their identity and destiny, were not taken into serious account by the former Yugoslav authorities. There was no systematic approach to data gathering, collection of witness accounts, or attempts to note important historical details.

A terrible mystery has been decried—a city under the ice! From relevant sources, we learn that more than 5,000 Novi Sad residents were thrown under the ice into the Danube. The authors of the banned radio drama stated in the broadcast that they did not want silent memorial plates lined along the bank! I do not want them either. All of us need living testimonies to remind us that we have to be humane above all. The slaughter termed "Novi Sad Razzia" that forcibly extinguished the lives of the victims should constantly warn us about the deadly consequences caused by Fascist and Nazi ideologies.

The river beach Strand, the most beautiful river beach on the banks of the Danube. Pictured at left is the entrance to the strand in the last century.

On January 23 each year, a dignified memorial rally is held at Strand Beach, where ordinary citizens gather to pay tribute to the victims on the very spot where the Hungarian gendarmes and military formed a line from which they took victims one by one to the hole in the ice, shot them, and dumped their bodies into the frozen river. That practice represents a break with the silent gray memorial plates posted at the monument not inspired by the sufferings of the victims of the 1942 Razzia. Due to this citizens' initiative, the world began the uncovering of the authentic memories that testify to the magnitude of the Genocide known as the Novi Sad Razzia of 1942.

ETHNICITY OF IDENTIFIED VICTIMS OF THE NOVI SAD RAID

1,401 ethnic Jews have been identified

737 ethnic Serbs have been identified

65 ethnic Hungarians have been identified

42 ethnic Croatians have been identified

27 victims are descendants of mixed marriages

23 ethnic Germans have been identified

22 ethnic Russians have been identified

20 ethnic Slovaks have been identified

8 ethnic Slovenians have been identified

7 ethnic Ruthenians have been identified

6 ethnic Poles have been identified

4 ethnic Czechs have been identified

3 ethnic Bunyevatz community members have been identified

1 ethnic Romanian has been identified

1 person of Islamic faith has been identified

LIST OF IDENTIFIED SERBIAN, JEWISH AND OTHER FAMILIES EXTERMINATED IN THE NOVI SAD 1942 RAZZIA

Following are lists of family names, organized by the number of members killed during the Razzia.

40 members

Goldstein

39 members

Shlesinger

36 members

Weiss

32 members

Stain

29 members

Berger

28 members

Klein

26 members

Shosberger

24 members

Schpitzer

23 members

Kohn

21 members

Levinger

20 members

Shtark

18 members

Deutch

17 members

Fischer
Kraus
Milich
Weinberger

16 members

Moizes
Shenberger

15 members

Breder
Jovanovich
Raich

14 members

Petrovich
Holender

12 members

Bugarski
Gavrilovich
Handler
Joykich

11 members

Engel
Hajdu
Kacaf
Kolb
Schwartz

10 members

Bohm
Horvath
Lustig
Morgenshtern
Popovich
Roth
Rozenberg

9 members

Beck
Boshkovic
Braun
Epstein
Goldberg
Grinwald
Kerac
Kolarovich
Krishaber
Lazarevich

8 members

Brandeis
Ciltzer
Dimitrijevich
Engl
Hefter
Hegedish
Hirt
Kail
Lyuboyev
Mogin
Moyinski
Pataki
Stoykov

7 members

Bokor
Fridman
Froud
Hoffman
Kolarov ("Mashins")
Layner
Loebl
Mihaylovich
Pisker
Santo
Sepeshi
Straynich
Weinberg
Zhivanovich

6 members	5 members	4 members
Aisler	Bayer	Arnstein
Aleksich	Blau	Atanackovich
Erdesh	Dungyerski	Bayich
Feher	Gaydobranski	Božin
Franck	Iritz	Brozinsky (Brochansky)
Glak	Jovandich	Crnya
Grnya	Katich	Davidovac
Gross	Lederer	Gabor
Gutmann	Nikolich	Gaidushek
Halmosh	Ormosh	Grbich
Hayosh	Polachek	Havash
Herzog	Polak	Ivanchevitch
Krstich	Revesh	Ivanovich
Malbashki	Rozenstain	Kabilyo
Noiman	Sikla	Kapamadziya
Shenfeld	Sremchevich	Katona
Shtern	Teichner	Levenberg
Stainberger	Wermesh	Levy
Stankovich	Werthaim	Marberger
Trebich	Zeremski	Momchilovich
Wamoshy		Pavlovich
Zemanek		Prodanovich
		Reiter
		Rozentzvaig
		Schil
		Schmidt
		Shteltzer
		Stoyanovich
		Totovich
		Vukanovich
		Waydman
		Yarhi
		Zonenfeld

3 members

Adam
Balazh
Barany
Biller
Bokshan
Brukner
Budoshan
Dietrihstein
Dobanovachki
Felbapov
Feldman
Frantzisty
Fucks
Funk
Gelb
Goldberger
Goldman
Gombar
Gongya
Gubanov
Gubash
Hass
Hauser
Heht
Heller
Hertzl

Hirstain
Hirtsh
Hubert
Ivkovich
Kaldor
Keller
Kertesh
Keshanski
Kimelberg
Kish
Kostich
Kovach
Kritzler
Kuzmin
Lengyel
Letich
Levenberger
Lihtenberg
Lihtner
Markovich
Mayer
Mendelsohn
Milichevitch
Mitrovich
Moshkovich
Nikolov
Ofner

Panich
Pap
Popper
Protopopov
Rozenstein
Sabo
Salachanin
Samardziya
Saranda
Satler
Sekely
Shorsh
Shraiber
Singer
Slankamenatz
Steinbach
Stoykovich
Tchyurchitch
Tomich
Trifkovich
Ungar
Vamosh
Vasich
Wigenfeld
Wolf
Wukich
Yano

2 members

Abraham
Adamovich
Ajzenshraiber
Akopnik
Alimpich
Amidzich
Andrich
Antonich
Bahman
Balog
Basler
Baumgartner
Belyansky
Benedek
Bichansky
Bjelich
Brankovich
Brkich
Budishin
Buton De
Chobor
Crammer
Cvetkovich
Cviyanovich
Darvash
Dunđerov
Dyurich
Elenbogen
Eple
Erendiner
Farkash
Felmann

Filipovich
Flaishšmann
Frigyeshy
Frond
Gero
Glick
Gozony
Grinn
Grubor
Gyakovich
Gyisalov
Gyokich
Gyurichich
Gyurishich
Gyurovicg
Haberfeld
Hazanovich
Hesel
Hil
Hirshenhauser
Hirshfeld
Hohberg
Hubai
Ivanov
Ivichich
Ivkov
Izhak
Jurishich
Kahn
Kardosh
Karpov
Katzanski
Kerekesh

Knezhevich
Kraguly
Laitner
Laskafeld
Lazich
Liht
Lipkovich
Lutzovich
Mandel
Mandil
Manoylovich
Marcekovich
Marich
Marichek
Marinkovich
Mariyash
Medakovich
Metrash
Mihalyevich
Milichitch
Mirkovich
Mishitch
Moizes
Moysey
Muller
Naivrit
Nastasich
Novak
Novkovich
Orban
Oreshkovich
Palich
Pantelich

Papich	Scher	Vernachki
Pavkovich	Schlanger	Veselinovich
Pavlas	Sege	Vuchkovich
Politzer	Senderak	Vukelich
Polyachky	Shash	Vukovich
Radivoyevich	Shik	Weiner
Radojchin	Shimon	Wig
Radujkov	Shnaider	Winter
Rafai	Shpigler	Wisel
Raihenberg	Shpiler	Yaki
Ranchevich	Shpringer	Yakovlyevicg
Rayich	Shuput	Yankovich
Regulashev	Skandarsky	Yefremovich
Reiner	Stanich	Yosikov
Ripp	Starchevich	Yoyich
Rosenfeld	Stoyadinov	Yugovac
Rosinger	Stoyakov	Zhagar
Rosinger	Stoyshin	Zhakich
Rozen	Tely	Zhivanov
Sass	Vadas	

1 member

Abonyi
Adler
Agyansky
Almoslino
Ambruster
Antoniyevich
Apich
Arsenin
Arsenov
Astahov
Atiyas
Babich
Bachich
Bachinatz
Bachvansky
Bakayich
Baky
Balshetz
Banyatz
Barechy
Barudziya
Bashich
Bashtovanov
Bauer
Baumgarten
Baykich
Becker
Bein
Bekvalac
Berkovich
Berlet
Birn
Birnberg–Weinberger

Bobich
Bodo
Bognar
Borosh
Borovac
Boshkovich
Boykich
Bozhidar
Brankov
Brayer
Brzak
Bubany
Buhbaum
Buhwald
Bulich
Buterer
Byro
Cayzel
Chalenich
Chasar
Chenche
Cheneyac
Chilag
Chippo
Chobanov
Chobansky
Chokich
Chovich
Chura
Churushki
Ciprik
Cipris
Crveni
Dachich

Dachin
Dadich
Dalnoky–Weresh
Daniel
Danilovich
Davidovich
Denesh
Deutch–Dalnok
Devich
Devichin
Deyanovich
Dimich
Dimitrov
Dmitrov
Dohany
Doroslovachky
Dozler
Dragich
Dragin
Draginchich
Dragoylov
Dragoylovich
Dragunovich
Drakulich
Drashko
Drashkovich
Drazhetin
Dronova–Spitzer
Dubachek
Dudak
Dulich
Dulyevatz
Dumnova
Dusa

Edelstein
Ekstein
Elenberg
Engelsmann
Erdelyan
Erenfeld
Eresh
Ernst
Ertl
Eshkert
Farago
Farbash
Fatzko
Fedotova
Fekete
Feldesh
Ferko
Flaisch
Flus
Fodor
Fraifeld
Freuel
Friderer
Fridland
Fridlender
Füller
Gachash
Gakich
Gal
Garbach
Gayger
Georg (Đorđe)
Gere

Gerich
Getz
Goldhamer
Gontzov
Goynich
Grahor
Grginchevich
Gruby
Gruyich
Gutvain
Gyerich
Gyorgyevich
Gyukich
Gyurin
Gyurishin
Hadler
Hadzich
Halashi
Hayling
Hebl
Hernfeld
Herzog
Hesser
Hirschler
Hirshl
Hodosh
Holberg
Horak
Hoydler
Hristich
Husit
Ibishich
Ignyatov

Ilesh
Ilich
Isakov
Ivich
Jakob
John
Kaderle
Kalmann
Kaplarovich
Katz
Kaufer
Kende
Kenigshtetler
Klauber
Klim
Kohn
Kokotovich
Koledin
Kolmann
Kolt
Komarchevich
Konich
Koruga
Kosirovich
Kovachich
Kraitmar
Krchmar
Krgin
Krizhanich
Krnetich
Krnyayich
Krumes
Kuhar

Kulashinovich	Mesarosh	Nishevich
Kurzak	Mezei	Novakov
Kuslich	Mikulinac	Novakovich
Kuyundzhich	Miladinovich	Novidzien
Lalich	Milenkovich	Obradovich
Lampel	Milichev	Obrenov
Lang	Milivoyev	Obushkov
Laslo	Milovanovich	Obushkovich
Latich	Milutinovich	Odrzhel
Laubert	Minta	Ograyenshek
Leh	Miok	Ogrizovich
Linder	Mirich	Ortstein
Lotz	Mirkov	Ostoyin
Lovchan	Mishkov	Pandurovich
Luchich	Mishkovich	Pandurova
Lukich	Mishlyenovich	Pantich
Lyuboyevich	Mitovich	Papkovich
Madatzcki	Molnar	Pardovitzki
Maksich	Molyac	Paroshky
Maksimovich	Molyk	Paulik
Maleshev	Momirovich	Paunich
Manigodich	Moshtrokol-Bilogoric	Pavich
Maravich	Moyatz	Pavichich
Marchek	Muha	Payich
Markovich	Murgashky	Pazalya
Markus	Nagy	Pekich
Marogyi	Nagyvinsky	Petrichich
Maryanovich	Nas	Petrovchanin
Masnec	Nemet	Petzarsky
Matanovich	Neshich	Petzich
Matich	Niderlender	Peyich
Mayechin	Niketich	Pihler
Mentzel	Nikolin	Pilischer

Pintar

Plachkov

Plavshich

Podvinetz

Polovina

Polyachky

Popov

Potochnich

Pratner

Preradovich

Prokich

Pruzhanov

Radashin

Radenovich

Radosavlyevich

Radovatz

Radovich

Rakich

Raletich

Ranchich

Ranisavlyevich

Rankovich

Rasheta

Ratkov

Raytcer

Reinmann

Relich

Reps

Revai

Rex

Rigyitzky

Rogulya

Rosenblit

Rosler

Rozenshtock

Rozha

Rozo

Rubanov

Rubovic

Rukshtein

Rushkutz

Rutka

Sablyica

Samardzicg

Samocheta

Sarafiloski

Savich

Savin

Sazdanich

Schadt

Shtrebich

Schwaiger

Sechenyi

Seizel

Sementovskiy

Shelb

Shikora

Shilich

Shiparov

Shmolka

Shogorov

Sholeogyi

Shtainic

Shtrangarov

Shtraser

Sigety

Simeunovich

Simich

Simin

Simitovich (Velykovich)

Sirova

Skopal

Slavnich

Slimag

Slotter

Smilyanich

Smilyansky

Spasoyevich

Srbin

Srdanov

Srpkich

Stanisavlyevich

Stankov

Stanoyevich

Starich

Stayich

Stefanovich

Stoyadinovich

Stoyakovich

Stoyich

Strayin

Strayinich

Streling

Striber

Suvaydzich

Svilokos

Syryshky

Talko

Tallo

Tambornino	Uvalich	Wainfeld
Tankosich	Uzelac	Wasermann
Tapavitzky	Valdner	Winterfeld
Taus	Valter	Wolberg
Temerinac	Valuh	Wolvorich
Tenyi	Valushek	Yakich
Teodor	Vaneasher	Yakov
Teshich	Varga	Yankelovich
Tivarov	Vasilyevich	Yankov
Todorovich	Vasin	Yankulov
Todosiyevich	Vidakovich	Yanyich
Toman	Vikentije	Yovichin
Tomash	Vitrael	Yugovich
Tomashevich	Vladovich	Yuhas
Tomlyanovich	Vlashkalich	Yukus
Torgl	Vlaykov	Yurlina
Toshich	Vogel	Zbunovich
Toth	Voznesenskiy	Zdravkovich
Tratner	Vranyeshevich	Zelinger
Trivkovich	Vrbashky	Zelyić
Trninich	Vrnchich	Zemunatz
Tzirich	Vrtunski	Zhikich
Tzorich	Vukshich	Zinger
Urban	Vürtz	Zucayich
Ushkuratz	Vuyich	

LIST OF IDENTIFIED MAIDEN LAST NAMES AND DESCENDANTS OF FEMALE LINES SHOT IN THE NOVI SAD RAZZIA

Abinun (1 person)
Adam (1 person)
Adamovich (3 persons)
Adamovich or Matich (1 person)
Aibenshitz (2 persons)
Aisman (7 persons)
Alinchich (3 persons)
Altenburg (4 persons)
Atanatzkovich (1 person)
Bader (2 persons)
Banchich (1 person)
Bash (2 persons)
Bayich (1 person)
Beck (12 persons)
Behm (5 persons)
Belgrader (1 person)
Berger (9 persons)
Berich (1 person)

Berkovich (1 person)
Blau (1 person)
Boginyev (1 person)
Bokor (2 persons)
Bonish (6 persons)
Boshan (1 person)
Boshnyakovich (5 persons)
Boskovic (1 person)
Bozhich (3 persons)
Brandeis (3 persons)
Brankovan (1 person)
Braun (1 person)
Braunfeld (4 persons)
Breder (5 persons)
Breiner (2 persons)
Broner (2 persons)
Bruck (1 person)
Brzak (4 persons)

Bubolyak (1 person)

Buhwald (4 persons)

Bukin (1 person)

Burg (3 persons)

Chanadi-Kovach (3 persons)

Chelinovich (2 persons)

Chokich (1 person)

Chordar (1 person)

Churski (1 person)

Ciltzer (3 persons)

Crveni (1 person)

Dekanich (1 person)

Deutch (4 persons)

Dimich (3 persons)

Dimitriyevich (1 person)

Dimovich (2 persons)

Dobanovachky (2 persons)

Dolovac (1 person)

Dorofeyeva (1 person)

Doroslovatz (1 person)

Dosler (4 persons)

Dragoylov (1 person)

Drenyak (1 person)

Drndarski (1 person)

Duhanek (1 person)

Dukas (1 person)

Dumnova (1 person)

Dun gyrsky (4 persons)

Dyorgyevich (1 person)

Dyukich (3 persons)

Dzigurski (1 person)

Elbert (2 persons)

Elezich (6 persons)

Engl (3 persons)

Epstein (3 persons)

Erdelyi (1 person)

Ergelashev or Miodragovich (1 person)

Ernst (2 persons)

Estehaimer (2 persons)

Faitman (3 persons)

Farkash (6 persons)

Fedotova (1 person)

Feit (3 persons)

Fekete (6 persons)

Feldman (1 person)

Felisher (1 person)

Filko (2 persons)

Fillinger (1 person)

Finner (4 persons)

Fisch (1 person)

Fischer (27 persons)

Fligel (2 persons)

Fodor (1 person)

Fraifeld (1 person)

Franck (3 persons)

Frankl (1 person)

Fratucan (2 persons)

Frenkl (1 person)

Freund (2 persons)

Frid (12 persons)

Fridman (4 persons)

Gabrish (3 persons)

Gavansky (3 persons)

Gayin (1 person)

Gelb (3 persons)

Gins (1 person)

Ginsberger (1 person)

Glasner (5 persons)

Goldberg (3 persons)

Goldman (5 persons)

Goldner (2 persons)

Goldstein (3 persons)

Golubich (1 person)

Gotzl (1 person)

Gradinac (2 persons)

Gross (6 persons)

Grunwald (2 persons)

Gruyich (1 person)

Gutman (4 persons)

Gyokich (1 person)

Haberfeld (2 persons)

Haim (2 persons)

Haintz (4 persons)

Handler (1 person)

Hauser (2 persons)

Hausler (1 person)

Hayosh (2 persons)

Hazanovich (2 persons)

Hefner (1 person)

Heller (2 persons)

Hernfeld (5 persons)

Hever (1 person)

Hexner (3 persons)

Hirn (1 person)

Hirschfeld (4 persons)

Hirshel (3 persons)

Hirshenhauser (3 persons)

Hofmann (3 persons)

Holender (2 persons)

Horvat (1 person)

Hoshan (1 person)

Hristich (1 person)

Hubert (3 persons)

Husar (1 person)

Ilich (1 person)

Iric (2 persons)

Ivanov (1 person)

Ivanova (1 person)

Izhak (2 persons)

Kaf (2 persons)

Kalany (1 person)

Kasovic (6 persons)

Kaufmann (4 persons)

Keller (2 persons)

Kellerman (3 persons)

Kenig (3 persons)

Kerac (1 person)

Kertesh (4 persons)

Kirnfeld (1 person)

Kiurski (2 persons)

Klein (16 persons)

Klopper (1 person)

Kohn (4 persons)

Kolarov (2 persons)

Kolarov-Mashin (2 persons)

Kolarsky (2 persons)

Kolb (8 persons)

Komlosh (3 persons)

Kondoroshy (3 persons)

Konrad (1 person)

Konstantinovich (3 persons)

Kopchansky (1 person)

Korn (3 persons)

Kostich (1 person)

Kostner (3 persons)

Kovach (6 persons)

Kovachevich (3 persons)

Kozlov (1 person)

Kozyak (1 person)

Kraus (8 persons)

Kristir (3 persons)

Kriyashin (1 person)

Kronstein (3 persons)

Krstonoshich (2 persons)

Lalich (1 person)

Lang (2 persons)

Laskafeld (7 persons)

Laubert (1 person)

Lederer (4 persons)

Leitner (13 persons)

Lendler (3 persons)

Letich (2 persons)

Levenberg (6 persons)

Levinger (2 osobe)

Levy (13 persons)

Lihtner (9 persons)

Lipkovich (5 persons)

Loebl (4 persons)

Loshic (1 person)

Lotbrein (1 person)

Lotz (2 persons)

Lustig (4 persons)

Maksimovich (3 persons)

Maletin (1 person)

Malka (4 persons)

Mandelbaum (5 persons)

Manhein (2 persons)

Marich (1 person)

Marinkov (1 person)

Markov (2 persons)

Markovich (2 persons)

Mautner (3 persons)

Mayer (2 persons)

Mezei (1 person)

Miklushvich (1 person)

Milich (3 persons)

Milko (1 person)

Milrat (1 personosoba)

Milutinovich (1 person)

Mirkovich (4 persons)

Mishkovich (2 persons)

Mogin (10 persons)

Moizes (4 persons)

Momirovich (2 persons)

Morgenst

Moyichich (2 persons)

Mrazovac (2 persons)

Nag (6 persons)

Naiburg (4 persons)

Nayfeld (1 person)

Nedeljkov (3 persons)

Neshich (3 persons)

Nikolich (2 persons)

Noihauz (1 person)

Novta (1 person)

Nusbaum (1 person)

Obrenov (1 person)

Ognyanovich (5 persons)

Openhaimer (1 person)

Ostoyich (1 person)

Palhedyi (1 person)

Palkovlyevich (1 person)

Paroshki (1 person)

Pashchan (5 persons)

Pashich (1 person)

Pavkov (1 person)

Pavlica (2 persons)

Pavlovich (1 person)

Pavlovski (1 person)

Peshar (1 person)

Peter (3 persons)

Petrovich (7 persons)

Petzich (3 persons)

Peyak (1 person)

Pirkeli (1 person)

Pisker (7 persons)

Plachkov (5 persons)

Plavshich (3 persons)

Plom (2 persons)

Polak (5 persons)

Pop Yovanov (1 person)

Popov (2 persons)

Popovich (1 person)

Popper (7 persons)

Presl (7 persons)

Pretzlmayer (4 persons)

Protich (2 persons)

Puhalek (1 person)

Purach (1 person)

Radich (2 persons)

Rado (1 person)

Rakich (4 persons)

Rakidzich (1 person)

Ralkov (3 persons)

Reger (1 person)

Reich (7 persons)

Reihenstain (2 persons)

Reiner (3 persons)

Reiter (3 persons)

Reitzer (5 persons)

Ripp (2 persons)

Ristovich (1 person)

Roder (1 person)

Rokich (2 persons)

Romano (1 person)

Rosenberg (3 persons)

Rosenhold-Rosenfeld (1 person)

Rosenshtok (3 persons)

Rosler (3 persons)

Rot (3 persons)

Roter (2 persons)

Rotfeld (4 persons)

Ruf (3 persons)

Sabo (1 person)

Sadetzkiy (1 person)

Samlaich (3 persons)

Santo (2 persons)

Savich (2 persons)

Savkov (1 person)

Schah (2 persons)

Schenberger (7 persons)

Scher (2 persons)

Schefer (11 persons)

Schik (6 persons)

Schkuch (3 persons)

Schlesinger (15 persons)

Schpitzer (12 persons)

Schtadler (1 person)

Schtark (4 persons)

Schtekl (1 person)

Schturk (1 person)

Schwartz (5 persons)

Sege (3 persons)

Sekulich (2 persons)

Senderak (2 persons)

Shenfeld (1 person)

Shiyachich (2 persons)

Shlanger (4 persons)

Shosberger (5 persons)

Shpira (2 persons)

Shraiber (3 persons)

Shtaynitz (3 persons)

Shteinbach (4 persons)

Shtesel (3 persons)

Shtosel (3 persons)

Shtrangarov (3 persons)

Shtrasser (1 person)

Shulyatzki (4 persons).

Shvayger (1 person)

Silashi (1 person)

Silber (8 persons)

Singer (8 persons)

Skopal (2 persons)

Slankamenactz (1 person)

Spayer (4 persons)

Sremchevich (1 person)

Stankovich (3 persons)

Stayich (1 person)

Stefanovich (1 person)

Stein (8 members)

Steinberg (4 persons)

Steinberger (5 persons)

Stern (9 persons)

Tagleught (5 persons)

Tarayich (3 persons)

Teltz (3 persons)

Tenner (4 persons)

Teodorovich (2 persons)

Teshitch (1 person)

Tiosavlyevich (8 persons)

Todorov (1 person)

Topalovich (1 person)

Torbarov (2 persons)

Trajfeld (1 person)

Tschurchin (1 person)

Tschurchiya (2 osobe)

Tscinkodi (3 persons)

Tuha (1 person)

Ungar (4 persons)

Uroshev (1 person)

Vadas (6 persons)

Valdner (1 person)

Valentin (4 persons)

Vamoshy (1 person)

Velgyi (2 persons)

Velich (6 persons)

Vernachky (1 person)

Vesich (3 persons)

Vig (6 persons)

Vilichich (1 person)

Voynovich (1 person)
Vrbashky (3 persons)
Vukichevich (6 persons)
Vukovich (1 person)
Weinberger (4 persons)
Weiner (2 persons)
Weinfeld (2 persons)
Weiss (21 persons)
Wolf (2 persons)
Yakovlyeva (1 person)
Yakshitch (4 persons)
Yefremovich (1 person)
Yelenich (8 persons)

Yelinek (2 persons)
Yoshinovich (1 person)
Yosimovich (2 persons)
Yovanovich (2 persons)
Yoyich (1 person)
Yoyin (1 person)
Zaborovski (2 persons)
Zaharova (1 person)
Zaloscer (3 persons)
Zemanek (1 person)
Zhikich (6 persons)
Zhivanov (1 person)
Zhivanovich (1 person)

A bust on display in Hungary, to Horthy's honor

ACKNOWLEDGMENTS

I will never forget the tireless support of Nenad Strainovic, the only person in Serbia who has stood by me at all times. He was a great inspiration to me, and the web genius who set up my Internet page.

Several of my former educators have my deepest gratitude for the role they have played that led up to this work: history teacher Michael Carter, who recognized my talent for historical research and provided encouragement, when, in 1992, he wrote of one of my history papers, "You have the workings of a great mind. Keep using it." I did not understand at that time what he meant; Stephen Allen, my biology teacher, for his unwavering support of my Holocaust and genocide research, which he considers important for humanity at large; Dr. David Maas, my former English linguistics teacher, and Dr. Jenai Rasmussen, my former political science teacher, for the knowledge they imparted to me and their ever-inspiring support for all of us who love the true history of our nations; and Mladen Bulut, a journalist from Novi Sad who unwaveringly stood by all my research and helped publicize it.

Special thanks to the first buyer of the first English edition, Micheal Lentz, and to all the other faithful readers worldwide, who have stood by this work in spite of all the opposition, blockades, and impediments that we have encountered on our way to the truth.

Above all, families of the victims, respecters of the victims of genocide and Holocaust, and all those who will read this book owe ultimate gratitude to the altruists at Something Or Other Publishing, whose vision and commitment to this historical truth has made it possible for the second English edition to now see the light of day. They have believed that this historical narrative bears a great significance for humankind.

NOTES

SECTION I

CHAPTER 1

1. *Vojna Enciklopedija*, vol. 3 (Belgrade, 1973), p. 430.
2. Those were the words of Hungarian Prime Minister Pal Teleky, which he spoke to a French general. Teleky's words were quoted in the book *Admiral na belom konju* by Milos Ćorović (Belgrade: Narodna knjiga, 1981), p. 29.
3. Miloš Ćorović, *Admiral na belom konju* (Belgrade: Narodna knjiga, 1981), p. 30.
4. "Srpski Narod u Mađarskoj," *Položaj i perspektive srpskog naroda u zemljama okruženja*, ed. Miodrag Jakšić and Simon Đuretić (Belgrade: JP "Službeni glasnik," 2009). (Taken from an article published in 2009 under the auspices of the Serbian Ministry for Diaspora.)
5. Milisav R. Đenić, *Zlatibor u prošlosti* (Titovo Užice: b.i., 1983), p. 84.
6. Randolph L. Braham, *The Politics of Genocide: The Holocaust in Hungary* (Detroit: Wayne State University Press in association with the United States Holocaust Memorial Museum, 2000), p. 23.
7. Đenić, *Zlatibor u prošlosti*, p. 84.
8. Braham, *The Politics of Genocide: The Holocaust in Hungary*, p. 21.
9. Braham, *The Politics of Genocide*, pp. 21-22.
10. Braham, *The Politics of Genocide*, p. 23.
11. Ćorović, *Admiral na belom konju*, p. 32.

CHAPTER 2

1. Danilo Urošević, *Srbi u logorima Mađarske* (u Barču i Šarvaru 1941–1945) (Novi Sad: Papirus, 1995), pp. 10–11.

2. *Godišnjak Društva istoričara SAP Vojvodine* (Belgrade: Društvo istoričara SAP Vojvodine, 1974), p. 207.

3. Miloš Ćorović, *Admiral na belom konju* (Belgrade: Narodna knjiga, 1981), p. 73.

4. Randolph L. Braham, *The Politics of Genocide: The Holocaust in Hungary* (Detroit: Wayne State University Press in association with the United States Holocaust Memorial Museum, 2000), pp. 24–25.

5. Đorđe Vasić, *Hronika o oslobodilačkom ratu u južnoj Bačkoj* (Novi Sad: Savez udruženja boraca NOP Srbije za Vojvodinu, 1969), pp. 25–26.

6. Horthy's letter to Hitler was published in *Zbornik dokumenata i podataka o narodnooslobodilačkom ratu naroda Jugoslavije*, vol. 15, book 1 (o učešću Hortijeve Mađarske u napadu i okupaciji Jugoslavije 1941–1945) (Belgrade: Vojnoistorijski institut, 1986), p. 15.

7. Srbija u ratu i revoluciji 1941–1945, Grupa autora—Redaktor Dr. Jovan Marjanovic (Belgrade: Srpska književna zadruga, 1976), p. 471.

CHAPTER 3

1. A testimony of a World War II veteran, Dr. Milan Runić, interview by author on June 9, 2008, in Novi Sad.

2. Runić, A testimony of a World War II veteran.

3. Runić, A testimony of a World War II veteran.

4. *Vojna Enciklopedija*, vol. 3 (Belgrade, 1973), p. 430.

5. Đorđe Vasić, Hronika o oslobodilačkom ratu u južnoj Bačkoj (Novi Sad: Savez udruženja boraca NOP Srbije za Vojvodinu, 1969), p. 30.

6. *Izabrani Spisi* (Novi Sad: Muzej socijalističke revolucije Vojvodine, 1974), p. 372.

7. Vojvodina u Narodnooslobodilačkom ratu i socijalističkoj revoluciji *1941-1945* (monograph), ed. Čedomir Popov (Novi Sad: Filozofski fakultet, Institut za istoriju, 1984), p. 47.

8. Rastislav M. Petrović, *Zavera Protiv Srba* (Belgrade: Književnoizdavačka zadruga Dositej), 1990, p. 192.

9. *Zapisnik Komesarijata za izbeglice i preseljenike u Beogradu od 20. februara 1942.* [Translation: A note by the Commission for Refugees and Displaced Persons in Belgrade, written on February 20, 1942.]

10. *Izveštaj Pokrajinske komisije za utvrđivanje zločina okupatora i njihovih pomagača u Vojvodini* (Novi Sad, 1946), pp. 278-283. [Translation: A report by the Regional Commission for Establishing [the facts about] the War Crimes of Occupiers and Their Collaborators in Vojvodina]

11. *Vojvodina u Narodnooslobodilačkom ratu i socijalističkoj revoluciji 1941-1945* (monograph), Čedomir Popov, Ed. (Novi Sad: Filozofski fakultet, Institut za istoriju, 1984), p. 47. [Translation: *Vojvodina in the People's Liberation War and Socialist Revolution 1941-1945*]

12. Danilo Urošević, *Srbi u logorima Mađarske* (u Barču i Šarvaru 1941-1945), (Novi Sad: Papirus, 1995), p. 16.

13. Urošević, *Srbi u logorima Mađarske*, p. 17.

14. Urošević, *Srbi u logorima Mađarske*, pp. 17-18.

15. *Izveštaj Pokrajinske komisije za utvrđivanje zločina okupatora i njihovih pomagača u Vojvodini* (Novi Sad, 1946), pp. 278-283. [Translation: *Report of the Regional Commission for Determining Crimes of the Occupiers and Their Collaborators in Vojvodina*]

16. Urošević, *Srbi u logorima Mađarske*, pp. 13-14.

17. *Izveštaj Pokrajinske komisije za utvrđivanje zločina okupatora i njihovih pomagača u Vojvodini*, p. 110.

18. Vladislav Rotbart, *Ne zaboravi druga svog: hronika o tamnovanju i borbi rodoljuba iz Bačke u segedinskom zatvoru* (1941-1944) (Novi Sad: Institut za izučavanje istorije Vojvodine, 1976), p. 338. [Translation: *Do Not Forget Your Comrade: Chronicle of the Imprisonment and Struggle of Patriots from Bačka in the Szeged Prison*]

19. Rotbart, *Ne zaboravi druga svog*, p. 5.

20. "Izveštaj Svetozara Markovića o gubicima komunističke partije od aprila 1941," do oktobra 1942, godine (published in *Izabrani spisi*, Svetozara Markovića, Novi Sad, 1974, p. 372).

21. Državna komisija za utvrđivanje zločina okupatora i njihovih pomagača, Saopštenje broj [no.] 89: *Zločin prinudnog regrutovanja stanovništva Bačke i Baranje od strane mađarskih okupatora*, Belgrade, 1946. [Translation: State Commission for Determining Crimes of the Occupiers and Their Collaborators, Statement number 89: *Crime of Forced Recruitment of the Population of Bačka and Baranja by Hungarian Occupiers*, Belgrade, 1946.]

22. Državna komisija [no.] 89: *Zločin prinudnog regrutovanja*.

23. Državna komisija [no.] 89: *Zločin prinudnog regrutovanja*.

24. Državna komisija [no.] 89: *Zločin prinudnog regrutovanja*.

25. Državna komisija [no.] 90: *Zločin prinudnog regrutovanja*.

26. Državna komisija [no.] 89: *Zločin prinudnog regrutovanja*.

27. A testimony by Sinisa [Simon] and Agneza [Agnes] Kaludjerski, given to the author on November 7, 2007, about the war stories related to them by their late next-door neighbor, an ethnic Hungarian.

28. Državna komisija [no.] 89: *Zločin prinudnog regrutovanja*.

29. Državna komisija [no.] 89: *Zločin prinudnog regrutovanja*.

30. Rotbart, *Ne zaboravi druga svog*, p. 6.

31. Živko Paunić, *Sećanje na ratne dane 1941-1945* (Novi Sad: Istraživački i tehnološki centar, 1997), p. 189-191.

32. Paunić, *Sećanje na ratne dane 1941-1945*, pp. 192-196.

33. Paunić, *Sećanje na ratne dane 1941-1945*, pp. 197-204.

34. Paunić, *Sećanje na ratne dane 1941-1945*, pp. 205-206.

35. Državna komisija [no.] 89: *Zločin prinudnog regrutovanja*.

36. Državna komisija [no.] 90: *Zločin prinudnog regrutovanja*.

37. Jaša Romano, Jevreji Jugoslavije 1941–1945: žrtve genocida i učesnici *NOR* (Belgrade: Savez jevrejskih opština Jugoslavije), 1980, p. 157.

38. Državna komisija [no.] 90: *Zločin prinudnog regrutovanja*.

39. Državna komisija [no.] 90: *Zločin prinudnog regrutovanja*.

40. Milorad Ćurčin, *Putevima Slobode u ravnici* (Žabalj: Savez udruženja boraca NOR, 1974), pp. 503-504.

41. Jaša Romano, Jevreji Jugoslavije 1941–1945: žrtve genocida i učesnici *NOR* (Belgrade: Savez jevrejskih opština Jugoslavije, 1980), pp. 157-158.

42. Urošević, *Srbi u logorima Mađarske*, p. 23.
43. Urošević, *Srbi u logorima Mađarske*, p. 23.
44. *Izabrani Spisi* (Novi Sad: Muzej socijalističke revolucije Vojvodine, 1974), p. 354.
45. Urošević, *Srbi u logorima Mađarske*, p. 26.
46. Urošević, *Srbi u logorima Mađarske*, pp. 11-12.
47. Miloš Lukić, Žedničke iskre: hronika Novog Žednika, (Novi Sad: Institut za istoriju, 1978), p. 434.
48. Ćorović, *Admiral na belom konju,* p. 182.
49. *Izveštaj Pokrajinske komisije za utvrđivanje zločina okupatora i njihovih pomagača u Vojvodini* (Novi Sad, 1946), pp. 52-67. [Translation: *Report of the Provincial Commission for Determining the Crimes of Occupiers and Their Collaborators in Vojvodina*]
50. Urošević, *Srbi u logorima Mađarske* pp. 83-84.
51. *Zbornik dokumenata i podataka o narodnooslobodilačkom ratu naroda Jugoslavije (o učešću Hortijevske Mađarske u napadu i okupaciji Jugoslavije 1941-1945)*, vol. 15, book no. 1 (Belgrade: Vojno-istoriski institut Jugoslovenske armije, 1986), p. 130. [Translation: *Collection of Documents and Data on the People's Liberation War of the Peoples of Yugoslavia*]
52. *Srbija u ratu i revoluciji 1941-1945* (monograph), Grupa autora—Redaktor Dr. Jovan Marjanovic (Belgrade: Srpska književna zadruga, 1976), p. 472. [Translation: *Serbia in War and Revolution 1941-1945*]
53. Ćorović, *Admiral na belom konju,* p. 183.
54. *Vojvodina u Narodnooslobodilačkom ratu i socijalističkoj revoluciji 1941-1945* (monograph), ed. Čedomir Popov (Novi Sad: Filozofski fakultet, Institut za istoriju, 1984), pp. 66, 70-71. [Translation: *Vojvodina in the People's Liberation War and Socialist Revolution*]
55. Izveštaj Pokrajinske komisije za utvrđivanje zločina okupatora i njihovih pomagača u Vojvodini (Novi Sad, 1946), p. 56.
56. Državna komisija [no.] 89: *Zločin prinudnog regrutovanja*.
57. Državna komisija [no.] 90: *Zločin prinudnog regrutovanja*.
58. *Pesti Hirlap*, December 17, 1941 edition. (Hungarian daily newspaper)

59. Urošević, *Srbi u logorima Mađarske*, p. 31.

60. Lukić, *Žedničke iskre: hronika Novog Žednika*, pp. 435-436.

61. Urošević, *Srbi u logorima Mađarske*, pp. 36-37.

62. Urošević, *Srbi u logorima Mađarske*, p. 38.

63. Urošević, *Srbi u logorima Mađarske*, pp. 39-40, 45-46.

64. Urošević, *Srbi u logorima Mađarske*, p. 46.

65. Urošević, *Srbi u logorima Mađarske*, pp. 49-51.

66. Urošević, *Srbi u logorima Mađarske*, p. 52-53, 55.

67. Urošević, *Srbi u logorima Mađarske*, p. 56.

68. *Đorđe Vasić, Hronika o oslobodilačkom ratu u južnoj Bačkoj* (Novi Sad: Savez udruženja boraca NOP Srbije za Vojvodinu, 1969), p. 32. [Translation: *Đorđe Vasić, Chronicle of the Liberation War in Southern Bačka*]

69. Tosli Vlado njilatkozata. N F M Adattara AK. 87.5.

70. A testimony of Branislav Milić given to the author on April 15, 2009, in Novi Sad.

71. Urošević, *Srbi u logorima Mađarske*, p. 57.

72. Urošević, *Srbi u logorima Mađarske*, p. 60.

73. Urošević, *Srbi u logorima Mađarske*, p. 61-63.

74. Urošević, *Srbi u logorima Mađarske*, p. 63.

75. Urošević, *Srbi u logorima Mađarske*, 64-65.

76. Lukić, *Žedničke iskre: hronika Novog Žednika*, p. 439.

77. Urošević, *Srbi u logorima Mađarske*, p. 80.

78. Lukić, *Žedničke iskre: hronika Novog Žednika*, p. 439.

79. Lukić, *Žedničke iskre: hronika Novog Žednika*, p. 440.

80. Urošević, *Srbi u logorima Mađarske*, pp. 46, 59, 63, 79.

81. The data about the consequences of the Hungarian occupation of Transylvania originated with a Romanian historian, Spalaceu (published in *Admiral na belom konju* by Miloš Ćorović, p. 79).

82. Excerpts from Horthy's letter to Hitler were published in *Admiral na belom konju* by Miloš Ćorović, p. 101.

83. Državna komisija [no.] 89: *Zločin prinudnog regrutovanja*.

84. Ćorović, *Admiral na belom konju*, pp. 109, 111.

85. Braham, *The Politics of Genocide*, p. 27.

86. Elek Karsai, *A Budai Vartol a Gyepuig, 1941-1945* (Budapest: Táncsics, 1965), pp. 203-206 (quoted in Braham, *The Politics of Genocide*, p. 58).

87. Ministries Trial (Court IV, Case XI), Veesenmayer's testimony on July 22, 1948, transcript p. 13243 (quoted in Braham, *The Politics of Genocide*, p. 60).

88. Braham, *The Politics of Genocide*, pp. 60-61.

89. Braham, *The Politics of Genocide*, p. 61.

90. Braham, *The Politics of Genocide*, pp. 55, 61.

91. Braham, *The Politics of Genocide*, p. 61.

92. Braham, *The Politics of Genocide*, p. 252.

93. Braham, *The Politics of Genocide*, pp. 252-254.

94. Randolph L. Braham with Scott Miller, eds., *The Nazis' Last Victims: The Holocaust in Hungary* (condensed edition), (Detroit: Wayne State University Press in association with the United States Holocaust Memorial Museum, 1998), p. 43.

95. Braham, *The Politics of Genocide*, p. 253.

96. Lukić, Žedničke iskre: hronika Novog Žednika p. 441.

97. The findings of the Hungarian historian Nemeshkirty were published in *Admiral na belom konju* by Miloš Ćorović, pp. 133-136.

CHAPTER 4

1. Vera Jovanović, *Slikar Bogdan Šuput (1914-1942)* (Novi Sad: Spomen- Zbirka Pavla Beljanskog, 1984), p. 170.

2. The figures for the January 1942 Razzia are taken from the database of Razzia victims at the Holocaust Memorial Society in Novi Sad.

3. "Avenge the Victims of the January Massacre in Backa" ["Osvetimo žrtve januarskih pokolja u Bačkoj"], *Slobodna Vojvodina*, year III, No. 8, January 25, 1944 edition, p. 2.

4. A testimony of Ivan Ninić, a relative of the Handler family, given to the author on August 19, 2007.

5. A testimony of Milijana Milićević, from Ribnica, given to the author in her home on October 13, 2007.

6. *Pesti Hirlap,* January 10, 1942 edition. [Hungarian daily newspaper]
7. Zbornik dokumenata NOR, vol. 1, book 17, p. 43 (quoted in Vera Jovanović, *Slikar Bogdan Šuput (1914-1942),* p. 170).
8. Quoted in Miloš Ćorović, *Admiral na belom konju* (Belgrade: Narodna knjiga, 1981), pp. 189-190.
9. *Godišnjak Društva istoričara SAP Vojvodine* (Belgrade: Društvo istoričara SAP Vojvodine, 1974), p. 210.

CHAPTER 5

1. *Godišnjak Društva istoričara SAP Vojvodine* (Belgrade: Društvo istoričara SAP Vojvodine, 1974), pp. 212-213.
2. Miloš Ćorović, *Admiral na belom konju* (Belgrade: Narodna knjiga, 1981), p. 203.
3. *Godišnjak Društva istoričara SAP Vojvodine* (Belgrade: Društvo istoričara SAP Vojvodine, 1974), pp. 212-213.
4. Ćorović, *Admiral na belom konju,* p. 8.

CHAPTER 6

1. "Srpski Narod u Mađarskoj," *Položaj i perspektive srpskog naroda u zemljama okruženja,* ed. Miodrag Jakšić and Siniša Đuretić (Belgrade: JP "Službeni glasnik," 2009), pp. 125-134.
2. Petar Lastić, "O Srbima u Mađarskoj," *Položaj i perspektive srpskog naroda u zemljama okruženja,* ed. Miodrag Jakšić and Siniša Đuretić (Belgrade: JP "Službeni glasnik," 2009), pp. 29-37.
3. "Srpski Narod u Mađarskoj," *Položaj i perspektive srpskog naroda u zemljama okruženja,* pp. 125-134.
4. Mirko Radonjić, "Opasne igre sa granicama u Evropi," *Večernjih novosti,* June 7, 2009.
5. "Saopštenja o zločinima okupatora i njihovih pomagača u Vojvodini 1941-1944," book 1, *Zločini okupatora u Vojvodini 1941-1945,* Pokrajinske komisije za utvrđivanje zločina okupatora i njihovih pomagača u Vojvodini (Novi Sad: Glavni Izvršni odbor Autonomne pokrajine Vojvodine, 1946), pp. 18, 19, 23, 328.

6.   Aleksandar Ignjatović, *Genocid u međunarodnom i nacionalnom krivičnom pravu* (Belgrade: Novinsko-izdavačka ustanova "Vojska," 1996), p. 15.

7.   Ignjatović, *Genocid u međunarodnom*, pp. 53, 81, 85.

8.   Ignjatović, *Genocid u međunarodnom,* p. 119.

9.   Zhilinsky's Memorandum to Horthy was published in its entirety for the Serbian public in *Racija-zaboravljen Genocid*, by Aleksandar Veljic (Belgrade: Metaphysica, 2007), pp. 300-322.

SECTION II

CHAPTER 1

1.   Shaikashka is a region in northern Serbia located in a triangle between the Tisa and Danube rivers. It has always been populated predominantly by Serbs; Serbian news clips and news reports from the 1970s contain information related to the Razzia and the strife of Endre Baichy Zhilinsky who claimed that 12,763 victims were murdered in January 1942 during the Razzia.

2.   Zhilinsky's Memorandum to Horthy was published in its entirety for the first time in Serbia in *Racija-zaboravljen Genocid*, by Aleksandar Veljic (Belgrade: Metaphysica, 2007), pp. 300-322.

3.   The Serbian translation of this German document was published in *Zbornik Matice Sprske za Istoriju*, vol. 35 (Novi Sad: Matica srpska, 1987), pp. 181-202. The translator Milan Ristović published the document under the title *Jedan nemački dokument o novosadskoj raciji januara 1942.*

4.   "Hungary Before the German Occupation," *Holocaust Encyclopedia* (online edition), United States Holocaust Memorial Museum: http://www.ushmm.org/wlc/en/?ModuleId=10005143.Accessed between January 6, 2011, and January 3, 2012.

5.   *Zbornik dokumenata i podataka o učešću Hortijevske Mađarske u napadu i okupaciji Jugoslavije 1941-1945*, vol. XV, book 1 (Belgrade:

Vojnoistorijski institut; Budapest: Vojnoizdavačka organizacija „Zrinji"; 1986), p. 509. [Translation: *Collection of Documents and Data on the Participation of Horthy's Hungary in the Attack and Occupation of Yugoslavia 1941-1945*]

CHAPTER 2

1. These figures are based on collected data about the Razzia victims stored in the Holocaust Memorial Society's database in Serbia.

2. Andrija Deak, *Pod žutom trakom* (Belgrade: Prosveta, 1953), p. 118. Note: Andrew Deak also published his memoirs in English and German as *Razzia in Novi Sad* (Zürich, 1967).

3. "Avenge the Victims of the January Massacre in Backa" ["Osvetimo žrtve januarskih pokolja u Bačkoj"], *Slobodna Vojvodina*, year III, No. 8, January 25, 1944 edition, p. 2.

4. Dragoslav Ognyanovich, *Children of the Rebellious Plain* [Dragoslav Ognjanović, *Deca buntovne ravnice*] (Novi Sad: Institut za istoriju, 1984), p. 117.

5. Vera Jovanović, *Slikar Bogdan Šuput (1914-1942)* (Novi Sad: Spomen- Zbirka Pavla Beljanskog, 1984), p. 140.

6. Pokrajinska komisija za utvrđivanje zločina okupatora i njihovih pomagača u Vojvodini, *Zločini okupatora i njihovih pomagača u Vojvodini protiv Jevreja (Istrebljenje, deportacija, mučenje, hapšenje, pljačka)*, (Novi Sad, 1946), p. 83. [Translation: Regional Commission for Determining the Crimes of Occupiers and Their Collaborators in Vojvodina, *Crimes of the Occupiers and Their Collaborators in Vojvodina against Jews (Extermination, Deportation, Torture, Arrest, Plunder)*]

7. Lazar Rakić, *Nadalj (do 1945. godine)*] (Novi Sad: Matica srpska, 1988), pp. 218-219.

8. Živan Kumanov, Bačka u narodnooslobodilačkoj borbi: kratak pregled, Novi Sad, 1960.

9. Đorđe Vasić, Hronika o oslobodilačkom ratu u južnoj Bačkoj (Novi Sad: Savez udruženja boraca NOP Srbije za Vojvodinu, 1969), p. 160.

10. Gyjuritza Labovich and Peter Razhnatovich, *Resistance of Defenseless in Concentration Camps* [Đurica Labović i Petar Ražnatović, *Otpor Golorukih Kroz Logore*] (Belgrade: Grafika, 1970), p. 177.

11. Milorad Ćurčin, *Putevima slobode u ravnici* (Žabalj: Savez udruženja boraca NOR, 1974), pp. 252-253, 461-462.

12. Laza M. Kostić, *Srbi i Mađari u XIX i XX veku (fragmenti)*, vol. 7 (Toronto: Srpski kulturni centar "Sveti Sava," 1975).

13. Đoko Slijepčević, *Jugoslavija uoči i za vreme Drugog svetskog rata* (Munich: Djoko Slijepčević, 1978), p. 292. Quoted in this work is an excerpt from the German version of Horthy's memoirs: Nikolaus von Horty, *Ein Lieben für Ungarn* (Athenaeum Good, 1953), pp. 240-241.

14. János Buzasi, *Az ujvidéki Razzia* (Budapest: Kossuth Könyvkiadó, 1963), p. 91.

15. Paul Shosberger, Jews in Vojvodina: a brief overview of the history of Jews in Vojvodina [Pavle Šosberger, *Jevreji u Vojvodini: kratak pregled istorije vojvođanskih Jevreja*] (Novi Sad, 1998), pp. 180, 300-401.

16. Jasha Romano, *Yugoslavian Jews in 1941-1945, Victims of Genocide and Participants of the National Liberation War* [Jaša Romano, *Jevreji Jugoslavije 1941-1945: žrtve genocida i učesnici NOR*] (Belgrade: Savez jevrejskih opština Jugoslavije, 1980), p. 160.

17. *Vojvodina in the Liberation War and Socialist Revolution 1941-1945*, book 25 [Vojvodina u Narodnooslobodilačkom ratu i socijalističkoj revoluciji 1941-1945, knjiga 25].

18. Ivan Ivanyi, *Games on the Banks of Danube*, John Cox's translation from German to English (Internet publication). Note: Ivan Ivanji gave a testimony to the author about this figure which he published online as *Games on the Banks of Danube* (translated from German by John K. Cox and posted at http://wordswithoutborders.org/article/games- on-the-banks-of-the-danube). The online excerpt comes from Ivan Ivanji's work "Spiele am Donaustrand," *Die andere Seite der Ewigkeit: Zwanzig Geschichten vom Tod* (Vienna: Picus, 1993), pp. 58-62.

19. "A World War II Nazi Discovered," *Public Voice*, Sept. 30, 2006, Internet edition ["Pronađen nacista iz Drugog svetskog rata," *Glas javnosti*, 30. septembar 2006].

20. *Izabrani spisi* (Novi Sad: Muzej socijalističke revolucije Vojvodine, 1974), p. 358.

21. Zločini okupatora i njihovih pomagača u Vojvodini protiv Jevreja (Istrebljenje, deportacija, mučenje, hapšenje, pljačka), Pokrajinska komisija za utvrđivanje zločina okupatora i njihovih pomagača u Vojvodini (Novi Sad, 1946), p. 83.

22. Vladislav Rotbart, *Jugosloveni u mađarskim zatvorima i logorima 1941-1945* (Novi Sad: Dnevnik, 1988), p. 63.

23. For years, the Holocaust Memorial Society in Serbia has been defending the veracity of Hungarian sources claiming that at least 12,763 individuals were murdered in the Razzia in 1942.

CHAPTER 3

1. *Dnevnik Vladimira Popovića*, p. 66 (from a diary written on a typewriter).

2. Miroslav Antić, *Spomenik*, 1967 (film).

3. Petar Jovanović and Dubravka Valić, *Radio drama Racija: januar 1942*, Novi Sad, 1986 (announcers: Ratko Radivojević and Loran Prokopić, music Willy Gregec, ton production Ivan Fece).

CHAPTER 4

1. *Zapisnik 15. marta 1943. godine u Komesarijatu za izbeglice i preseljenike u Beogradu: iskaz Vere Sotirović*, stare 32 godine, supruge Stavre Sotirovića, kapetana jugoslovenske vojske iz Novog Sada, izbeglička legitimacija broj 118570.

2. Miloš Lukić, *Nemirno ognjište: zapisi iz prošlosti Sremske Kamenice* (Novi Sad: Savez udruženja boraca NOR SR Srbije za Vojvodinu, Razzia, murdered on January 22, 1942).

3. Testimony of Eržebet Pap-Reljin, a renowned TV documentary producer, the granddaughter of Janos Szabo's sister, given to the author on December 8, 2008.

4. Igor Mihaljević, "Život i bekstvo Novosađanke Hermine Dajč tokom januarske racije 1942. godine," Novi Sad daily *Dnevnik*, April 10, 2007 edition, Novi Sad.

5. Testimony of Leah Wasserman, *nee* Pessing, given to the author on June 27, 2007.

6. Testimony of Lea Ljubibratić, given to the author on April 26, 2010.

7. Testimony of Lazar Isakov, given to the author on May 18, 2010.

ABOUT THE AUTHOR

Aleksandar Veljic, translator, researcher, and writer, was born in 1971 in Belgrade. In 1990, he graduated from Sixth Belgrade High School with a librarianship major. While staying with relatives in London, who offered refuge and support during the civil war in the former Yugoslavia, he studied at Francis King School of English in 1992, and later attended Ambassador College in the United States, majoring in English literature.

Upon returning to Serbia in 1996, Aleksandar embarked on a close examination of the little-known World War II crimes committed by the Nazi Germans and their allies in the former occupied Yugoslavia. His painstaking research has resulted in several works on the genocide against Serbs, Jews, Roma, Slovaks, Ruthenians, Slovenes, Russian emigrants, and anti-Fascists of German, Hungarian, and other descent. In 2008, he and the members of the Holocaust Memorial Society discovered a forgotten Holocaust site in the Serbian village of Perlez.

Aleksandar Veljic is also the author of a successful handbook on basic English grammar for Serbian students. He is the founder and president of the Holocaust Memorial Society. In March 2023, Aleksandar Veljic founded the Hope of Israel Worldwide Church of God with the objective to spread the good news of the coming supernatural deliverance from antisemitism, hatred, and conflicts in humanity.

www.ingramcontent.com/pod-product-compliance
Lightning Source LLC
Chambersburg PA
CBHW060052100426
42742CB00014B/2787